Water in the Garden

FRONTISPIECE

A small informal pool with a natural-looking rock formation behind, well decorated with plants.

Water in the Garden

by

DOUGLAS BARTRUM

JOHN GIFFORD LIMITED
125 CHARING CROSS ROAD
LONDON WC2

First published 1968

© Douglas Bartrum 1968

Printed in Great Britain
by Billing & Sons Limited, Guildford and London

Contents

		Page
Preface		7
Introduction		9
Chapter		
1	Brooks and Streams	19
2	Riverside Gardens, Springs and Bogs	39
3	Lakes, Ponds and Pools	53
4	Some Hardy Water-lilies	62
5	Some Tender Water-lilies	73
6	The Giant Water-lily and Some Other Kinds	81
7	Pools for the Garden	87
8	Planting and Decorating	105
9	Making a Bog-garden	118
10	Fountains and Cascades	135
11	Japanese Water-gardens	144
12	Some Fish for the Pool	151
13	Some More Plants for Pools and Water-gardens	156
	Bibliography	168
	Index	169

PREFACE

WATER supplies in most gardens usually come in the form of rain. And with tanks connected to the guttering round the house we can catch it and use it, perhaps to supply a small fountain (as described in Chapter 10, page 136, of this book). More often than not, however, the only source is the kitchen-tap which we turn on to fill or replenish a Water-lily pool or a Goldfish pond. How many gardens have a stream running through them or a natural pool fed by fresh spring water? Most of us would have to think hard to try to remember where we saw a small private garden so well supplied by nature. The aim of this book is to give advice to gardeners who want an artificial piece of water of some sort in their gardens. It may be a concrete pool or a fountain or perhaps a cascade flowing into a pool.

Water-gardening on the whole is less arduous nowadays, for we can buy prefabricated pools and sink them into the ground. They are not as deep as the concrete kinds we make and therefore not able to accommodate many of the largest and loveliest Water-lilies. But most of them are the right size for the average modern garden – and quite deep enough for many charming aquatics and certain kinds of Goldfish.

Special chapters are devoted to the description and cultivation of aquatics, both the ornamental and the useful kinds. Water-lilies and Goldfish (usually the two together) come first with most of us; and they thrive best when they have the support of oxygenators and floating aquatics, about which, many gardeners know very little. Information is given about the value and use of these in Water-gardens.

One thing not mentioned in this book is danger from water in the garden. The matter isn't mentioned in any books on Water-gardening I have read. Yet there is danger where there is a depth of water exposed in a garden; young children should not be allowed to wander unattended near a pool. It is possible of course to drain pools and ponds and it is sometimes a good plan to do this at the end of the season. Plants grown in containers (as they often are these days) are easily removed and kept in a

7

cold greenhouse till the following spring when they are put out again.

In a book this size it is impossible to include all the plants that are suitable for growing in a Water-garden. The Royal Horticultural Society's Dictionary gives a comprehensive list of Water Plants, and I have chosen some of the most useful from it and from other suitable genera described in the main body of that work.

It is hoped that *Water in the Garden* will serve as a source of information for gardeners who want to make an ornamental pond or pool and are looking for plants to grow in it and round it.

D. B.

Marlow, Bucks

INTRODUCTION

'No garden is complete without water.' So said a famous landscape gardener – 'water' meaning anything from a natural stream to a small artificial pool, or even half a barrel sunk in the ground for tiny Water-lilies.

There aren't many gardens with natural pools or springs or with streams running through them. In some valleys there are riverside gardens, but these are usually ordinary gardens with a river frontage, the river being part of the landscape – a natural feature – which has nothing to do with the garden proper.

It is possible of course to utilise the water (if one can get the necessary permission), and make a canal to run through the garden and empty itself into an artificial lake or pool. This was done at Gyldenscroft, Marlow-on-Thames, many years ago, the canal being used for boats to take people from the house for outings on the river. (The great attraction, by the way, was the gondola and the gondolier, both imported from Venice.) At Greengates near Henley-on-Thames there is a long river frontage to the grounds, and where it is low, with the water occasionally rising and lapping it, Bog Primulas, mostly *Primula japonica*, are planted and have seeded themselves in the moist soil. Unfortunately some of these places suffer from flooding and during the winter much of the ground is under water.

A riverside garden, however, is not strictly speaking a Water-garden. The true Water-garden is an integral part of the garden, and may be a pool or a stream suitably planted with aquatics.

Many people have been puzzled by the term. What actually is a Water-garden? Charles J. Cornish in *The Naturalist on the Thames* (1902) gives one definition, viz., 'A recent addition to the country house is the Water-garden, in which a running brook is the centre and *motif* of the subsidiary ornaments of flowers, ferns, shrubs, and mosses.'

It isn't a garden in itself, of course, but a feature like the herbaceous-border, or the rockery. ('Rock-garden' is a comparable term.) A garden which was practically all water, stepping-stones and aquatic plants would be as monotonous as one which was all rocks and alpines.

One of the finest in the country (it is fed by water in the surrounding slopes) is at the Savill Gardens, Windsor; the streams run through the main part of the grounds and provide the right situations and the perfect setting for the aquatics grown.

The 'running brook' type of water-garden is rare – there aren't many gardens which have a brook running through them. But there are other types: the formal, for instance, whose *motif* is a rectangular pool or it might be described as a miniature canal. (I have seen them 12 feet long by about 3½ feet wide, in quite small gardens.) A fairly shallow ledge built round the edges, inside, and filled with soil contains the plants: things like the Flowering Rush (*Butomus umbellatus*) and *Iris kaempferi*, which flourish luxuriantly in a few inches of water.

Most people, however, who want water in their gardens make a simple pond and leave it at that. It has no pretensions to a Water-garden; a Water-lily is planted in the middle and it is referred to as the Lily-pool or the Goldfish pond. And the artificial pool (which is sometimes a sunk tub) is a popular feature in gardens today.*

Pool or pond? We usually speak of a Lily-*pool* and of a Fish-*pond* (Goldfish pond). The Lily-pool in this country is not much more than a hundred years old but the Fish-pond, the economic Fish-pond with its fresh-water fish, dates from the Middle Ages or earlier. Every monastery had its piscina or Fish-pond. Fish, fruit and vegetables were more important to the community than flowers – except those that were used in the preparation of medicines.

Tracing the history of these two words, the O.E.D. gives first *Pool* (*c.* 897); a quotation from King Alfred's translation of 'Gregory's Pastoral Care'; then *Pond* (*c.* 1300).

And the definitions are: *Pool*. 'A small body of standing or still water, permanent or temporary: chiefly, one of natural formation.'

Pond. 'A small body of still water of artificial formation, its bed being either hollowed out of the soil and formed by embanking and damming up a natural hollow. Often described according to

---

* Many people are now buying the ready-made plastic pools or tanks, which are sunk into the ground.

its use, etc., ... as a compensation-pond (for a canal, etc.), duck-pond. . . . Formerly often specifically Fish-pond.'

But there was often little distinction between the two: 'Pool, or ponde for fysche kepynge.' (1440.) O.E.D.

Ornamental ponds became popular in our gardens when the hardy types of Water-lilies (*Nymphaea*) were introduced, which was about the middle of the nineteenth century. Before this, tender species like the blue, scented *Nymphaea caerulea* (from Africa: introduced in 1812) and *N. lotus* (the Lotus-lily of Egypt), 1802, were grown in greenhouse-tanks, the water being easily maintained at the correct temperature.

About 1880 the famous hardy Marliac hybrids were introduced by M. Marliac of Temple-sur-Lot, France. Pink, red, crimson, yellow, were some of the colours: these hybrids eclipsed our native white species, *N. alba*; and some were small enough for tubs: *N.* × *pygmaea helvola*, for instance: it has sulphur yellow flowers not much more than an inch across. (Similarly, Alpine-plants brought the rockery, the wall-garden and the moraine into our gardens – the trailing kinds, for example, were seen to best advantage on a rock-wall.)

It was in the hot-house pools at Chatsworth (Derbyshire) about the middle of the nineteenth century that the giant Water-lily *Victoria amazonica* (*V. regia*) was first flowered by Joseph Paxton, superintendent of the gardens at that time.

WATER FEATURES IN ENGLISH GARDENS

Chatsworth is an example of one of our great gardens which are famous for their ponds, fountains and various water devices. From the River Derwent flowing past, a canal was made and extended the whole length of the estate; it is figured along with the many fountain-ponds or basins in an old engraving by Kip, dated 1685.

This was the time of the lavish lay-out, when vast sums were spent by the nobility on canals, fountains, cascades, many of which were designed by landscape-architects from the continent. Grelly, from France, a pupil of Le Nôtre (d. 1700), planned the water devices at Chatsworth.

Hampton Court, the home of Cardinal Wolsey, dates from the sixteenth century and, like Chatsworth and other famous estates, has seen changes of style in the lay-out of its gardens.

Wolsey had the garden planned in the mediaeval English manner; and Henry VIII, who occupied the place after the Cardinal's death (1530), made considerable alterations, introducing many features in the Italian style. The so-called Old Pond Garden, a favourite spot with visitors, is not much different, however, in its basic plan, from the original of Wolsey's time – a tank for fish replaced what is now the circular Lily-pool.

Hampton Court was perhaps a link between the mediaeval castle- or fortress-gardens and the later renaissance gardens, whose grandiose lay-outs owed much to French and Italian influence.

Going further back to the Middle Ages, the castle-garden, with its moat and high walls, followed rather closely at first the plan of the monastery-garden, which is the earliest type of English garden known to us. Both castle and monastery had their fish-ponds (or fish-stews) and occasionally a bathing-pool. Henry III, 1207–1272, had a garden enclosed by walls made at Woodstock, Oxfordshire, for his spouse Eleanor of Provence, and gave instructions for an herbarium and a fish-pond to be built 'whereat the queen may be able to amuse herself.' And the pond was the feature of these early gardens that was preserved during the changes that occurred through the course of centuries. Many an estate built on the site of a mediaeval monastery can boast of its ancient fish-pond or piscina, which was later converted into a Fountain-basin or a Lily-pool.

The history of the ornamental garden-pool can be traced back, then, to the monastery pond, which was supplied by water from a well or a spring. Water was often brought from a nearby river to fill tanks in some gardens which had no natural supply; at Hampton Court, for instance, it came from the Thames; but usually in the grounds of a monastery there was a well enclosed within the walls.

What information we possess concerning the lay-out of these gardens is gleaned from ancient MSS and the beautifully executed miniatures that illuminate them. These MSS date from about the twelfth century. And our knowledge of gardens in Britain ceases at this period. We cannot go back any further. It is possible that the Romans, who had brought gardening to a high pitch of development in their own country, made canals and ponds for the irrigation of the soil in the parts of England they occupied, but in the excavations extant there is no evidence of this.

Irrigation is of less importance, of course, in our country, which enjoys a comparatively high rainfall, than it is in the hot dry countries of the South.

WATER FEATURES IN FOREIGN LANDS

Egypt, which is essentially an agricultural country, had several efficient systems of watering many centuries before the Christian era. The shadoof was a primitive contrivance used for raising water from the Nile for crops that were grown in elevated country. It is still seen today and consists of a horizontal pole working on a pivot, with a bucket at one end and a counterpoised weight at the other.

Ponds and canals were important features of the gardens and are figured in the fresco-paintings and reliefs that were discovered in the tombs and temples of the earliest dynasties.

In the tombs at Beni-Hassan, a village on the Nile, there are pictures of garden scenes dating from the XIIth dynasty (3000–2500 B.C.); one shows two gardeners bringing water in earthenware jars from a pond for plants growing in square, regularly-spaced beds. A narrow canal leads from the beds and terminates in the pond.

The palace gardens of Ikhnaton (Amenhotep IV) were famous for their ponds surrounded by flower-beds; and Rameses III (c. 1225 B.C.) grew 'rushes and the Lotus. . . .' (The Lotus is now considered to be *Nymphaea lotus*, with white and rose flowers.) Both plants needed water; and his gardens are described as having tanks and ponds for Lotus-flowers.

The Lotus-pool was an ornament of many gardens in the countries where the plant grew wild. In India, Ceylon and China it is the Nelumbo (*N. nucifera* or *N. speciosum*, the East Indian Lotus), with fragrant, pinkish-white flowers and leaves which do not float but are supported on stems standing well above the water. The earliest garden-designers of the East were quick to appreciate the decorative value of the plant and grew it in the ponds and basins they built in the gardens attached to temples and palaces. In the *Mahavamsa*, a Cingalese chronicle of great antiquity, we read that a palace garden 'had many ponds, whose borders were decked with beauty, lovely with the abundance of Lotus and of Lilies. . . .' In these hot countries water also had a more elemental use: large sunk canals or cisterns, often of white marble, were made and filled with water from a spring to give a feeling of coolness and repose to the garden-scene.

The long canal in the Court of the Myrtles at the Alhambra Gardens, Granada, is a magnificent example. The canal, edged with stone pathways and flanked on each side by a formally-clipped Myrtle hedge, runs the whole length of the enclosed court. And at one end a tall building with battlements is reflected in the unbroken surface of the water.

The most famous example of the beauty of the reflected image in water is perhaps at Agra (India). Constance Villiers-Stuart mentions it in her book *Spanish Gardens*, where she describes the canal in Indian gardens: 'The canal gains in width with the passing of the centuries until by the time that the Taj Mahal (at Agra) was built, it is broad enough to reflect in its tranquil waters the full beauty of the buildings at each end . . .' (The Taj Mahal dates from the middle of the seventeenth century.)

Many of the bridges built over the lakes and canals in Chinese gardens are arched (the arch a perfect semicircle), the reflected image combining, as it were, and giving the complete circle, which is so satisfying to the eye of the viewer.

The little bridge of white marble and stone crossing the narrow canal in the garden of Li-Ching-Mai, Peking, is built in this manner. Chinese poets and writers often found inspiration in the tranquil beauty of things reflected in water. The great lyricist Li Po (A.D. *c.* 705–62) in *The Porcelain Pavilion* writes:

> And in the lake the little bridge appears
> A crescent moon of jade, turned upside-down;
> So standing on their heads our friends are seen
> In lightest garments clad, and drink their wine
> In a porcelain house.

Very little is known of the earliest gardens of China; but paintings from the later dynasties show many garden-scenes, which seem to our eyes often more quaint than beautiful. Rocks and stones are piled up in strange disorder; there are artificial hills or mounds of earth, with a pavilion or some other building on the top of the highest; and there is always a pond or a running stream.

Similarly in Japanese gardens in ancient times there was usually a piece of ornamental water; it was often a pond or a lake which was designed to represent the shape of an animal or a bird. (See chapter 11, page 144.) Sometimes earth was heaped up in the background to form a miniature hill and was dotted about with those curious, gnarled dwarf trees, which for centuries the Japanese have cultivated so skilfully.

Many of the finest gardens in China and Japan are those attached to temples and monasteries. The Buddhist monks (in both countries) fostered the art of gardening, as did the monks in the West, and laid down the principles which the later designers adapted to suit their own particular needs. Water and bridges were among the most important features; in the luxurious gardens of the *daimyo* (ancient feudal Lords), when there was no water and for some reason it could not be brought into the garden, it was suggested by a meandering pathway of sand with stones embedded in it, or by overhanging trees.

There is no evidence of gardens in ancient Greece till the Homeric and the Hellenistic ages. The Homeric epics describe groves planted near temples; and the nymphaeum, a grotto-like feature, with trees and running water. No doubt the rocky, precipitous nature of the country made the wide planning of gardens impracticable, but in the cities, in Athens, for example, there were large pleasure gardens with shady seats, cooling fountains and streams. (See chapter 10, page 135.)

Excavations have brought to light various interesting facts about the plants cultivated and the gardens made by the peoples of these old civilizations; and the writings extant give us more specific information. To the Geoponici (eminent Greek and Roman writers on agricultural subjects) we are indebted for the descriptions of some magnificent Villa-gardens. Pliny (A.D. 23–79) had a Villa at Tusculum (15 miles SE of Rome), where there were 'basins and streams of water, partly for ornament and partly for irrigation . . .' (*The History of Garden Making*, ed. by Charles Holme).

In the Middle Ages, when Italy was torn with wars between the Goths and the Byzantines, the Church proved a bulwark of the arts. The monks planned and cultivated their gardens as they did in mediaeval Britain. And it was not till the dawn of the Renaissance that landscape architects began to design gardens on the same lavish scale as those of the early classical period.

There are magnificent examples of their work in Rome and Florence. The Palazzo Vecchio at Florence is celebrated for its fountain and laughing cherub (the latter the work of the Florentine sculptor Andrea del Verrocchio, 1435–1488), originally at the Villa Careggi.

Italy is famous for its fountains, those of the Renaissance Villas, such as the Villa d'Este, Tivoli, being among the most elaborate ever designed. Other water features – cascades, pools and the egregious 'water-tricks,' which spouted water in the faces of the unwary stroller – have always been a source of delight to visitors.

The French soon began to imitate the Italians. Charles VIII (1470–98), who took Naples in 1495, was greatly impressed by all he saw in Florence and Rome and brought back with him artists and a Neapolitan gardener Passello da Mercogliano, to whom he entrusted the task of beautifying the royal estate at Amboise, a town on the Loire, in N.W. France.

The Renaissance influence spread through Europe. The Italian style and the baroque (late sixteenth century) were much admired by the rich land-owners of the north, many of whom had seen the Villa gardens in Italy and introduced features in the Italian style, especially fountains and various water-devices, into their own gardens. For the most part, however, few alterations were made in the existing lay-outs; and the broad planning of gardens continued on traditional lines.

Spain is famous for its Water-gardens. The Moors designed the finest during their occupation of the country in the Middle Ages and thus introduced into Europe a new Oriental style of garden-design and ornamentation. The 'centre and *motif*' of these water-gardens was the canal. At Granada they built the Alhambra (the Court of the Myrtles, with its long canal is mentioned on page 14) and the Palacio del Generalife, the summer residence of the Moorish kings, where there are some magnificent examples of Moorish workmanship. The Garden Court at the Generalife, with its narrow canal and fountains flanked with tall Cypresses, is one of the show places of Southern Spain and dates from the fourteenth century.

At Toledo, a centre of Moorish culture till the eleventh century, the last ruling caliph had a pavilion built, with a remarkable water-device that threw water high into the air and spread it out in such a way that it fell again and surrounded the pavilion and its occupants completely. The cooling effect this produced must have been much appreciated during the long hot summer seasons.

The Arab gardens of Morocco were planned specifically to provide places of rest and shelter from the tropical sun. So they were enclosed by high walls or buildings and usually paved with marble, and the canal, with a simple fountain – often a single jet of water – combined to make a cool secluded retreat.

This type of formal Water-garden is seen in Spain today and has been copied by landscape architects in many parts of the world. Most of them are comparatively small (they are planned for the average-sized villa) and necessarily more simple in design. Stone paving has replaced the marble, and the garden or court is usually enclosed by simple stuccoed walls.

It is the type of lay-out which will appeal to many people, for it is the essence of the labour-saving garden. Formal stone paving,* flagstones, for example, replace grass, which has to be regularly mowed, or gravel, which has to be weeded; and often the plants are grown in pots and stood round the canal as they are in Spanish gardens.

People living in towns or cities, where gardens are small and enclosed by walls, will find the lay-out particularly suitable; and it can easily be adapted to suit their needs; for instance, the canal may be used for Water-lilies and will be planned on a small scale (perhaps 6 feet in length and 2 feet in width) or a simple circular pool with a stone rim can be substituted for it.

The lay-out is hardly suitable, however, for the average garden in the country, which as a rule is much larger than the town-garden and seldom enclosed by walls. Boundaries are mostly fences, wooden or wire, or hedges, neither of which accords well with stone-paving: the one exception perhaps is the Yew hedge neatly clipped to a rectangular shape. (The long canal in the Court of the Myrtles at the Alhambra is flanked by clipped hedges, but these are purely decorative and subservient to the stone buildings immediately behind.) In the average garden the enclosed court, with its canal or pool, must be planned as a feature, like the Water-garden with its running brook. It is rather like the modern 'garden-room,' which adjoins the house

* Crazy paving would be quite out of place in the Spanish style of Water-garden.

– though this being roofed in can hardly accommodate a Lily-pool.

Fountains and cascades are seen in many gardens today; hitherto they were found only in the pleasure-gardens of the rich. (The great fountains and water-devices of the past were 'set-pieces' and essentially spectacular.) They are simple now and, like the canal and the ornamental pool, often designed and constructed by the owners of the gardens themselves. And in being simple – the single jet of water or the cascade flowing over a boulder – they best provide that feeling of repose and tranquillity which water should bring to the garden.

CHAPTER ONE

Brooks and Streams

THE IDEAL Water-garden is the natural one, with a running brook as the 'centre or *motif*.' Where the ground slopes gradually down to the edge of the water, there may be some flooding during a wet winter, but nothing like that which occurs in riverside gardens, when plants may be submerged for many weeks or even uprooted by the deep swirling water.

Brooks or streams are usually shallow. The water seldom rises very high. On the other hand, it may drop to an alarming extent during a prolonged drought and cause moisture-loving plants growing on the banks to wither and die. The remedy of course is to grow them at water-level and to plant them in a rich, leafy soil. I have in mind the lovely Candelabra or Asiatic Primulas. Some, the three-foot, yellow *Primula florindae* and the tiny pink *P. rosea*, for example, flourish luxuriantly when planted in shallow water in a semi-shady spot. It is not a difficult matter to dig away some of the bank to make a sort of bay where these choice plants can be grown.

A running brook is not suitable for Water-lilies. These need a stretch of still water in which to establish themselves. But people who are fortunate enough to have a brook in their gardens should certainly make use of it to provide water for a pool. I don't think it should be a formal pool, but one surrounded by foliage plants or some sort of semi-wild plants which would be in keeping with the natural lay-out and at the same time afford an agreeable contrast to the lilies.

A narrow canal or conduit coming from the brook will supply the pool with water, or pipes may be laid, which would perhaps be less trouble than excavating a canal, since this would have to be lined with cement.

The canal or pipes can also supply the water for cascades, or a waterfall, or a rivulet meandering through a rockery. It must be remembered, however, that the supply will naturally run short when the water begins to drop in the brook – and it may eventually dry up. Where there is the danger of this happening, the pool (especially where valuable Water-lilies are growing) must be replenished by means of the garden-hose. (The construction of pools is discussed in chapter 7.)

A brook running through an uncultivated piece of ground will have its banks covered with grass, and no doubt a variety of wild plants. And there may be some really decorative ones among them.

The loveliest we find by streams, in my opinion, is the Marsh Marigold (*Caltha palustris*), with large deep golden yellow buttercup-like flowers.

Its natural habitat is the edges of ponds and streams, and it will sometimes be found in shallow water. The double-flowered form *C. palustris* var. *plena* is offered by many nurseries and is even more beautiful than the single type; I have never seen it growing wild. It should be bought (Hilliers stock it), a dozen, if possible, and planted by the water's edge, in a sunny place. Give it a good rich loam, with an admixture of sifted leafmould, and plant it in early September, if possible, so that it can become established before the cold weather sets in. Propagation is by root-division or by seeds.

Forget-me-not (*Myosotis scorpioides*) is another native plant which will be found growing along the banks of streams. It does equally well in sun or shade.

Myosotis scorpioides semperflorens is a dwarf form which blooms all the summer – I don't care for the white variety *alba*.

The easiest way to grow these is to sow the seed in spring where the plants are to flower. Choose a spot, of course, where people are not liable to walk, and provide a moist peaty loam. (Both the Marsh Marigold and the Forget-me-not, by the way, can be grown in a shady corner, where the soil is a deep rich loam which doesn't dry out.)

Rumex hydrolapathum, best known as the Great Water Dock, is a magnificent foliage plant, which may be seen flourishing luxuriantly by ditches and streams and in damp places. I like it for the contrast it provides and for its decorative effect during the autumn when there is little in bloom. In some districts it is less common than either the Marsh Marigold or the Forget-me-not. Nurseries who specialise in hardy aquatics usually have it for sale.

The wild yellow Iris (*Iris pseudacorus*) is a waterside plant which occasionally grows in the shallow water of a brook or in marshy ditches; it seems to favour the deeper water of a river, however; its glaucous, sword-shaped leaves are handsome and make it a valuable foliage plant all through the year. The flowers come in early summer.

Where the garden is uncultivated or has been neglected for years, no doubt there will be a wide variety of wild plants growing along the banks of the stream; some, like those mentioned above, vie with any of our cultivated plants; but the majority (with small insignificant flowers: *Lychnis flos-cuculi*, Ragged Robin;* *Lythrum salicaria*, Purple Loose-strife, etc.) should be weeded out with the grass to make room for choicer things.

It may be as well to begin with a tree or two, for these will give the shade which is necessary for some of the choicest of all waterside plants, viz., the hardy Asiatic or Candelabra Primulas. And the finest tree for the waterside is undoubtedly the Weeping Willow, *Salix babylonica* or the hybrid *Salix × blanda*, which is hardier than the former. There is also another, the Golden Willow, *S. vitellina* Var. PENDULA, worth growing for the striking effect of its gold-yellow bark in winter. Any of these may be chosen for planting near the water; one must remember, however, that all of them will eventually grow into enormous wide-spreading trees 50 or 60 feet tall – two fully-grown specimens would in time probably cover a small brook and you wouldn't know it was there!

But in its young state the Weeping Willow doesn't take up much room and it won't look out of place by the side of a narrow brook. The branches can be pruned back if they spread out too far.

Weeping Willows are most striking in early spring or even in late winter when the buds begin to swell and the long trailing stems become a conspicuous golden-yellow. The colour gives an extraordinary warm, enlivening effect to the winter garden.

As regards cultivation, the trees should be planted in ordinary loam and they are best staked firmly till they are well rooted and established.

* There is a giant Ragged Robin, a hybrid, *Lychnis × haageana*, which is well worth growing.

A sapling Weeping Willow is one of the most graceful trees it is possible to grow in our gardens.

Another suitable tree is our native Birch, *Betula pendula* (the Weeping Birch or Lady of the Woods), with its slender, white-barked trunk and graceful pendulous branches. Trees and shrubs of this shape are very appropriate for growing near a stream or a pool, the water seeming to attract the long, hanging branches.

B. pendula attains about the same height as the Weeping Willow, but not being so wide-spreading, takes up much less room. Two planted as near as 3 feet apart (one a little behind the other) make a delightful picture on the bank of a stream.

The variety YOUNGII (known as Young's Weeping Birch) is a smaller tree, with more pendulous branches and a dome- or mushroom-shaped head. Having a wider, spreading top, it should be set farther back on the bank.

Var. PURPUREA has purple leaves; but for planting near water I prefer the type plant.

Most of the Poplars (*Populus*) thrive in moist or in wet soils; but they are more suitable for riversides and large country estates than for an average-sized garden.

Bamboos also like an abundance of moisture, but many spread rapidly and would in a short time probably overgrow the stream.

I imagine most people will choose the Weeping Willow; but there are of course many other suitable trees and shrubs: a short list should include two Alders, viz. *Alnus glutinosa imperialis*, with deeply-cut foliage; and *A. rugosa.*

Arctostphylos uva-ursi, a small, prostrate, spreading shrub, with pinkish flowers in small racemes.

Some Azaleas (included now in the genus *Rhododendron*). *R. nudiflorum* has fragrant, usually pink flowers and grows to a height of 6 feet, it blooms in May; *R. viscosum*, the 'Swamp Honeysuckle,' which has fragrant, white or pink flowers in July. It is about 6 feet tall.

Cornus alba, 'Swamp Dogwood', a white-flowered shrub up to 10 feet tall, of rampant growth – probably better for a lake; *C. stolonifera* similarly is more suitable for planting by lakes.

Erica tetralix, the Cross-leaved Heather.

Gaultheria, a genus of evergreen spreading shrubs, noted particularly for their decorative fruits.

Hydrangea macrophylla varieties.

Ledum groenlandicum, an evergreen shrub 3 feet tall.

Rubus arcticus, a dwarf pink-flowered Bramble.

Vaccineum corymbosum, Swamp Blueberry, and other species belonging to this genus; these shrubs (evergreen and deciduous) thrive under the same conditions as Heathers and Gaultherias.

Where should shrubs and trees be planted? First the trees. For a small stream running through a garden, say, an acre in extent, only one or two will be needed: a Willow on one side and perhaps a Birch on the other. They should not be planted directly opposite each other or their branches will soon become entangled. If it is a straight piece of water, it doesn't matter much where they are placed (so long as they are spaced wide enough apart). But where the stream twists and turns, a tree should be planted near or on one of the bends to emphasize it.

The flowering shrubs Azalea and Hydrangea, although lovers of ample moisture, should not be set too near the water edge. I think they look most effective planted in clumps and receding into the background. Both shrubs prefer partial shade.

SOME FLOWERS AND SOME FERNS

Among the best of the waterside flowers are the hardy Primulas. Most gardeners want to grow them and have tried them in shady places (where there has been no stream or pool) and by dint of keeping them well watered have succeeded in getting them to flower. But usually by late summer the foliage has withered and dried up and there is little left of the plants.

They need constant moisture round their roots; indeed many flourish most luxuriantly when planted in shallow water. They are not suitable for boggy ground, where the moisture is stagnant – they are often described in catalogues somewhat misleadingly as Bog Primulas – but they are excellent plants for the made garden 'bog', where the soil is specially prepared for them.

Primula sikkimensis is the Himalayan Cowslip which smells so delightfully of cinnamon. It was the first species I ever grew and, I thought, the most attractive. The yellow flowers (like a Cowslip's) come at the end of erect fleshy stems, up to 2 feet tall – with me they never went above a foot, for these plants had to be accommodated in ordinary soil. The dark shining green leaves form a rosette from which the stems shoot up, the dark green contrasting beautifully with the yellow flowers. I let my plants seed in the place where they grew. Seedlings as thick as mustard and cress sprang up the second year. Ordinary leafy, loamy soil was used – I had no waterside.

You need at least a couple of dozen plants to make a show; and by the side of a brook there will be plenty of room for a hundred. I would set them out in rows of 10 or 12 to make a good conspicuous clump. The charm of the graceful hanging flowers is seen to best advantage when the plants are massed in this way.

The species was introduced into English gardens from the Himalayas well over a hundred years ago and is still probably the most popular of the hardy Asiatic Primulas.

P. florindae is a giant Sikkimensis, discovered by Kingdon Ward in South-east Tibet, growing at an altitude of 12,000 feet. On the whole it has proved easier to grow than the smaller species and does well in deep rich loams in shady borders. Nurseries recommend it for the herbaceous border.

Its stems reach a height of 3 feet, when the plant is grown in shallow water; its flowers are similar in shape to those of *P. sikkimensis* and a sulphur-yellow colour. The largest leaves measure 8 inches in length, are ovalish in shape and a deep shining green.

It is one of the tallest of all the species we grow and should be massed on its own away from smaller types.

P. rosea is probably seen in our gardens more often than the other two species; and no doubt its carmine-rose colour is its great attraction.

It can be planted in shallow water; it is often only a few inches high when it first comes into bloom; the scapes, or stems, then grow longer and the leaves similarly attain their full length, the largest measuring 8 inches.

Like the other two species described, it needs shade; yet if grown in water, it will tolerate a fair amount of sun. It blooms in April, and the two Sikkimensis Primulas begin to open some weeks later. (I have seen *P. florindae* in full bloom during July.)

These three species need a leafy or peaty loam with an admixture of coarse sand. They do not like lime.

The following descriptive list contains species and varieties which are seen in many of our gardens; all the plants prefer a rich moist loam and are consequently ideal for the Water-garden.

P. bulleyana is one of the tall Candelabra Primulas (up to 3 feet, near water) and has deep orange flowers – most arresting when they are massed in semi-shade. Its habitat is the Lichiang Range, Yunnan (China). Forrest discovered it and introduced it about 1909.

P. cockburniana belongs to the same group but is scarcely as big as the preceding species. Its colour is dark orange-red, a rich colour which is best on its own. In fact this species should be isolated from any other flowering plant that blooms simultaneously and associated with Ferns or with some other moisture-loving foliage plants. It flowers in June and as it dies usually after two years seed should be kept and sown in pans during the spring.

P. helodoxa is another tall species – up to 3 feet in its habitat (Yunnan and Burma) and mostly about 2 feet under cultivation. The flowers, a rich golden yellow, come in superposed whorls (about 4) up the stems and are fully open by June.

Like many another species, *P. helodoxa* will seed itself if left undisturbed.

P. japonica is one of the easiest of all the species to grow, provided you give it a shady place. It increases naturally but produces many seedling with inferior colours. Only plants with well-defined shades should be kept; the inferior kinds should be dug up before they have a chance to contaminate the others or, of course, seed themselves. I have grown a pure white form and a genuine deep rose in an ordinary shady border; the soil was a deep, rich, leafy loam; watering was only necessary toward the end of the flowering-season – mid-June.

Two good forms advertised by most nurseries are MILLER'S CRIMSON and POSTFORD WHITE.

P. japonica will tolerate more sun when its roots are growing in water. A rose-coloured form used to grow in full sun on the riverbank at Greengates, Henley. A native of Japan, the species was introduced into England about 1870.

P. poissonii, a candelabra type, requires less shade than many other Primulas. The best forms have deep purple-crimson flowers with a yellow eye. A striking colour. Paler forms should be scrapped; they are usually a washy purple or an uninteresting magenta shade.

It comes from the provinces of Yunnan and Szechwan (China), where it grows to a height of 18 inches or so.

It seeds itself freely in moist places but, as with *P. japonica*, many of the seedlings won't be worth keeping. Good forms are best propagated by root-division.

P. pulverulenta is another tall species, as tall as the giant Sikkimensis (*P. florindae*). Its mealy stems, with their tiers of usually pink or red flowers, reach a height of 3 feet or more; the leaves are a good contrasting green colour, oblong in shape, the largest measuring 12 inches in length. A really choice plant for massing by the waterside, especially where the ground slopes gently upwards from the water's edge, which shows up the massed tiers of flowers to best advantage. (There is a magnificent show in the water-garden at the Savill Gardens, Windsor.)

The famous Bartley Strain, raised by Mr. G. H. Dalrymple of the Bartley Nurseries, has given us such reliable plants as 'Lady Thursby' and 'Ruby Crimson.' These forms, when they seed, mostly come true to colour.

P. pulverulenta is also the parent of several fine hybrids such as RED HUGH (a rich copper-crimson – reputed to be the most vividly coloured of all Primulas) and AILEEN AROON, a brilliant orange-scarlet; the other parent of these two is *P. cockburniana*.

P. pulverulenta, a native of West Szechwan, was discovered by Wilson and introduced in 1905. It is a favourite plant for the woodland as well as for the Water-garden.

The ideal place for all these Primulas is by the side of a brook, where the flowing water keeps the soil sweet and clean.

Astilbe is a genus of herbaceous plants with flowers which come in plume-like spikes or in branching panicles. They are sometimes called *Spiraea* by gardeners and have occasionally appeared under this name in catalogues. But they are two separate genera.

Astilbe need the same sort of soil as the Asiatic Primulas – a deep, rich, moist loam, well drained – but they should not be planted so close to the water and never in it; they do best in a shady position.

For my part, I like to see them massed on ground which slopes up from the water edge, the plants spreading out among distant trees, the latter not too closely planted, but there should be enough to provide shade from the hot sun. (*Astilbe* bloom in mid-summer.) Primulas and other things which like wet soil can be planted in front.

The foliage is often finely divided and toothed and a charming foil to the feathery panicles of flowers, which are usually pink or red, cream or white.

The most popular kinds are the hybrids known as *A.* × *arendsii*, named for Herr Georg Arends of Ronsdorf, who raised them by the crossing of the four species *astilboides*, *davidii*, *japonica* and *thunbergii*. They are offered by most nurseries; their average height is 3½ feet: the tallest I know is the pure white KING ALBERT, 5 feet or more.

If you plant them in the way I suggested (on a sloping piece of ground), begin with the deep colours, say, the dark crimson GRANAT; it has rich green foliage suffused with bronze and is 2–2½ feet tall. One needs a clump of three at least to give a good show. Behind it QUEEN ALEXANDRA, deep pink; or PEACH BLOSSOM, a paler pink; and in the background the creamy-white WHITE GLORIA or the pure white PROF. V. D. WEILEN. These, planted in clumps, should be enough to cover a good-sized piece of ground. The massed upright feathery panicles give a charming light graceful effect.

There are other varieties just as lovely. I recommend BETSY CUPERUS, white and pink, 4–5 feet; CERES, elegant feathery sprays, lilac-pink, 3 feet; FANAL, dark garnet-red flowers and bronzy foliage, 2 feet; GLORIA PURPUREA, deep-purple-rose, 3¼ feet; RHINELAND, clear pink, an early bloomer, 2½ feet.

Where a pathway runs parallel to the stream, say, 6 feet or so away from it, there will be a break in the massed flowers (where a wide piece of ground is to be covered); a more natural effect will be obtained if the same variety (same colour) is grown on both edges of the pathway.

Ferns, with their finely-divided leaves, are ideal for associating with Astilbes; for many revel in moisture and shade and need lime-free, rich peaty soil.

There are many well-known native species; among them *Blechnum spicant*, a special favourite with people who grow collections of hardy Ferns in their gardens. Its popular name is the Hard Fern, which appropriately describes the tough, dark green fronds and the sturdy habit of growth. It is evergreen, with the inner fronds erect and fertile and the outer ones sterile and spreading outwards. They vary considerably in length:

they may be 9 inches in ordinary loams, but twice as long in damp, peaty soils. Gardeners who grow it say it does as well in clay as in a peaty compost, and it needs deep shade.

Ferns are a perfect foil to most flowers, and I cannot think of anything more suitable to set near the big Asiatic Primulas (say, *P. florindae* or *P. pulverulenta*) than this elegant native species.

Two other native Ferns are *Dryopteris filix-mas* and *D. oreopteris* (both will be found in nurserymen's catalogues). The first, known as the Male Fern, is the most common of our Ferns, a very hardy plant, evergreen in warm counties, with fronds up to 3 feet long and 1 foot wide. It likes shade and ample moisture at the roots. It would overwhelm the smaller Primulas but is very suitable for associating with Astilbes. It prefers a light sandy leafy loam and needs a fair amount of room. Imposing in a clump and very effective planted in a drift or a row among the taller Astilbes. Nurseries supply a good number of varieties: I consider var. BOLLANDIAE, with deeply cut fronds, one of the most striking. Most catalogues quote these Ferns at three shillings each.

D. oreopteris is popularly known as the Mountain Buckler Fern; the plant is mostly found in mountainous places. Like the preceding species, it has several attractive varieties. Hillier offers the type plant: 'An elegant Fern for moist, shady places.'

Osmunda regalis is the Royal Fern, a noble plant when it grows in rich peaty loam near water, but not so tall and big in ordinary soils. By the side of a stream a well-established clump may go up to a height of 6 feet; in a shady border I have seen specimens not more than 18 inches high. The foliage in summer is a charming pale green and in autumn becomes tinted yellow and gold.

The Royal Fern thrives best in sunlight in wet situations and is thus one of the most suitable for associating with water-loving flowers such as the Bartley Strain of *Primula pulverulenta* and some of the tall Irises. There is a lovely variety, CRISTATA, with wide, beautifully crested fronds; and Var. GRACILIS, a slender Fern, whose young fronds are sometimes tinted.

Other species of hardy Ferns are described on pages 111–113. Most nurseries who specialize in herbaceous plants stock them.

Ferns and Irises give us two contrasting types of foliage: pinnate or finely-divided; and sword-shaped and erect, which look well together and provide interest during the autumn and winter when there are few flowers in bloom.

The Royal Fern and our native Yellow Flag (*Iris pseudacorus* – 3 feet tall) make a delightful association for the side of a stream.

I. pseudacorus doesn't seem to appear in catalogues; it is common enough along our river-banks and may be collected there. The bright yellow flowers come in clusters and bloom during May and June.

Another native species is *I. foetidissima* (called the Stinking Gladwyn), which has bluish-lilac flowers, and blooms at the same time as the other species. It may be grown near the water edge and needs partial shade. It makes an enchanting picture massed in a clump near the Sikkim Cowslip (*Primula sikkimensis*) with yellow flowers. This Iris is also ornamental in autumn and winter, when it carries a profusion of orange-scarlet seeds.

I. sibirica and its many varieties have rush-like leaves and tall, slender stems, which carry the flowers, small and purplish as a rule and numerous.

It will grow in shallow water and blooms in June; for edging a brook, it is superb. Plant a drift some 12 feet long by 3 feet wide of the pure white variety SNOW QUEEN, half in the water, half on the bank.

Hilliers list *I. sibirica* EMPEROR (bright purple); MRS. ROWE (pearly grey); MRS. SAUNDERS (dark blue); PERRY'S BLUE (sky-blue); SANGUINEA (reddish-violet); SNOW QUEEN; SUPERB (red violet-blue).

I. kaempferi and *I. laevigata* are two wonderful water-irises. Both are natives of Japan and eclipse in colour and size of flowers any other Iris in cultivation. They are more difficult to grow than any of the other kinds described (*I. kaempferi* especially so).

I. kaempferi needs moisture round its roots all through the spring and the summer (it is best grown in shallow water) but the rhizomes should be high and dry during the winter. Some method of draining the water away could no doubt be devised – a channel made or a simple system of damming.

I. laevigata, on the other hand, will flourish in water all through the year. The value, too, of these two species and their varieties is that they bloom later than the Yellow Flag and the Sibiricas. Many varieties of *I. kaempferi* begin to open in July.

It is worth visiting an Iris Nursery or a Botanical Garden to see these plants in bloom. The flowers, with their horizontal spreading petals, often measure 10 inches across and the colours range from white and cream, through pale lavender-blue to rich purple and crimson. The popular name of the plant is the Clematis Iris of Japan. The following are some of the best known:

ADONIS. Single. Mauve on a grey ground. 2½–3 feet.
ATTRACTION. Double. White edged with lavender. 3 feet.
CASSANDRA. Double. Creamy-white, touched with rose. 3 feet.
HYMEN. Double. Mauve, veined with blue. 2¼ feet.
JUPITER. Single. Grey-blue, veined with purple. 2¼ feet.
MATSU-NO-JU. Deep violet-blue. Double. Enormous flowers. 2½ feet.
MOONLIGHT WAVES. Double. White – a lovely flower, known as Gekko-No-Nami in Japan. 3 feet.
MORNING MIST. Single. White, tinted with blue. 2¼ feet.
PURPLE SPLENDOUR. Double. Deep purple. 2 feet.
RUBY. Double. Rose-purple. 2½ feet.
VIOLET QUEEN. Single. Violet. 3 feet.

Most of these are of Japanese origin.

Iris laevigata is related to *I. kaempferi*, the latter being distinguished from it by the prominent midrib of its leaves. And culturally, *I. laevigata* is less trouble, not resenting water round its roots all the winter. It grows about 2 feet tall, the flowers are a clear blue, and the leaves narrow and elegant.

There are several lovely varieties: I recommend the following two. *I. laevigata* var. *alba*, with white flowers; and ROSE QUEEN, which has pale rose-coloured flowers. The finest specimens I have seen have been growing in about 4 inches of water, about a foot from the edge of a stream.

The Japanese varieties of *I. kaempferi* are without a doubt the choicest of all the Irises we grow: there is no other water-side plant quite like them; but they may look out of place planted by the side of a brook where wild plants are growing. I personally would choose the Yellow Flag and perhaps some purplish or blue Sibiricas to go with these *I. kaempferi*.

We don't usually associate Red-hot Pokers (*Kniphofia*) with water-gardens and streams. Their erect, red and yellow flowers and rush-like leaves are well known and valued for the late summer show they give. The plants should be massed and, where

—*Photo H. Smith*

1   A large pond in a semi-mature garden, with a small waterfall entering on the left.

2

Iris laevigata, (blue-purple) growing in shallow water.

3

Polystichum setigerum (Fern).

the soil is light and sandy, they could be grown instead of Astilbes, which need a richer, peaty, lime-free soil.

K. uvaria is the type plant which has produced many good garden forms and hybrids. For a limited space this species is an ideal choice, since it doesn't go above 18 inches in height. It is a native of South Africa and blooms during late August and September.

The garden forms are taller. MOUNT ETNA, for example, is 5 feet and has scarlet flowers. NOBILIS is rich orange-red and reaches a height of 6 feet or more. CORALLINA is a hybrid between *K. macowanii* and *K. uvaria*, about 2 feet tall and has orange-red flowers during July and August. They should be planted fairly close together so that no soil is visible.

These late-blooming Red-hot Pokers will carry on the show begun in spring and summer by the Asiatic Primulas – which should be planted in the foreground.

Lychnis chalcedonica is often referred to as the brightest scarlet flower in the garden; it is such a hard colour, in fact, that it is difficult to place the plant satisfactorily in the garden. It likes moist boggy soil and partial shade and has been grown success-fully by the side of a stream, in company with the wild Male Fern (*Dryopteria filix-mas*) – no other flowers were planted. Yet as this *Lychnis* blooms in mid-summer (June to August), spring-blooming Primulas can be planted near it, for they will have faded long before the hard scarlet flowers open.

There is a double variety, *L. chalcedonica rubra plena*, which flowers about the same time.

L. × *haageana* is a giant Ragged Robin (a hybrid between *L. fulgens* and *L. coronata sieboldii*), which grows about a foot high and has scarlet and orange flowers about 2 inches across. A beautiful waterside plant. (See page 21.)

Lysichitum. The foliage of this plant reminds one of giant spinach leaves – shining green, with prominent mid-ribs: very striking all through the summer and the autumn when the flowers are past; these are like large Arums (a yellow spathe enclosing a tall, green-stalked spadix) and they appear before the leaves – about April as a rule. It is rare in gardens and never fails to astonish gardeners who see it for the first time. It must be grown near water and despite its exotic look it doesn't seem out of place planted at the edge of a stream.

The specific name of the plant is *Lysichitum americanum*; it is a

native of Western N. America, where it grows by rivers and is
propagated by the seeds which are washed downstream and
caught in the debris lodged against the banks.

Some fine specimens may be seen in the water-garden at the
Savill Gardens.

The white-flowered species *L. camtschatcense* is also there and
blooms a little later. This species is a native of Eastern Siberia
and of Japan.

Both plants can be increased by root-division.

Hilliers list the yellow form: 'the yellow bog-arum' (price:
about 10s. 6d.).

It is difficult to find a suitable plant to grow with it – it
blooms in April. I prefer to see the simple sword-shaped leaves
of the Yellow Flag near it.

Mimulus. The genus comprises various species which like
moist situations; and the one most often seen is the Monkey
Musk, *M. luteus* or its variety *M. luteus guttatus*. The type plant,
which has a wide distribution in the Americas, is naturalized in
Britain and will be found by the side of streams and growing in
shallow water. The small, yellow flowers, spotted at the mouth,
are quite a common sight. They are less striking than those of
the variety mentioned, which has yellow flowers spotted
purplish-brown. The leaves are ovalish and sharply toothed.
Both plants are obtainable from nurseries.

They bloom during the summer and are about 18 inches tall.
I prefer *M. ringens* (1–3 foot tall) with violet or white flowers; it
is a good species to grow in shallow water and is just as hardy
as the other two.

The most famous species is *M. moschatus*, known as the Musk,
with its delightful smell. It was naturalized in Britain but has
been lost – apparently since about 1914. The variety HARRI-
SONII has supplanted it; it has larger flowers but unfortunately
they are practically scentless. Both plants like damp shady
places. (See also page 50.)

Polygonum affine is a quick-spreading plant which I have grown
in woodland and wild places, where it carried narrow, rose-
pink flower-spikes about 6 inches long during the autumn. It was
consequently a useful plant to have in the garden. Its habitat is
the riverside banks of Nepal and the moist river fields of the
Himalayas. An excellent little Knot Weed for filling up empty
spaces along the bank of a stream.

4
Lily James
Brydon.

5
Lily Laydeberi
lilaced.

—Photo L. E. Perkins

6   A formal pond with paved surround.

7   Phyllitis scolopendrium. Var Crispum grande.   —Photo H. Smith

Ranunculus lingua grandiflora is the Water Buttercup, which has large yellow flowers on stems about 2 feet long and blooms during the summer. It will grow in water or in marshy ground and can be obtained from most nurseries.

The plant known to most gardeners as *Saxifraga peltata* is now described under the name *Peltiphyllum peltatum*. It is fairly common in gardens and usually occupies the front row of a border, spreading its handsome roundish leaves on to the pathway; the pink or white flowers come early during a mild winter – sometimes at the end of March – and appear before the leaves. When these have faded, the species is a fine foliage plant till the autumn frosts, the deeply-lobed leaves giving a touch of tropical luxuriance to the garden. The largest specimens I have ever seen were edging a brook – only a few inches away from the water.

Spiraea. Astilbes (see page 26) are often described by gardeners under the genus *Spiraea*. On the whole Spiraeas are larger plants and although one or two may be planted at the water edge, they are more suitable for higher ground. *S.* × *arguta* goes up to a height of 8 feet in good loamy soil. I single it out as the best of the early-blooming kinds. It has pure white flowers carried in clusters of from 4 to 8 along the stems and small, narrow pointed leaves about 1½ inches long. It would look top-heavy set among dwarfer plants like the Asiatic Primulas growing close to the water. (This Spiraea is a hybrid from *S. crenata*, *S. thunbergii* and *S. hypericifolia*.)

S. japonica ANTHONY WATERER is perhaps the most popular of all the garden forms; it has plumes of deep carmine flowers which, however, are often of poor quality in many gardens; the plant needs a good deep, rich loam. It blooms in July and is especially effective in a clump of three or more – such a clump will measure about 5 feet across and the height of this variety is from 4 to 5 feet.

S. thunbergii is a species about the same height and has thick clusters of stalkless, pure white flowers on the arching, twiggy stems in April. A native of China and Japan, it is also noted for its gorgeous tints in the autumn (orange, yellow, scarlet) and should be grown on that account.

Spiraeas, like Astilbes, give the most striking effect when they are grouped, say, 3 or 5 of the same kind, in a clump.

They need a well-drained soil, which is rich and loamy, and

B

can be propagated by root-division or by late summer cuttings.

The different types of plants I have described are but a few of the many hundreds that are suitable for, or amenable to, waterside planting. Kniphofias and Spiraeas are more frequently seen in borders and shrubberies than near running brooks but they are very beautiful there.

BRIDGES AND STEPPING-STONES

How wide is a stream or a brook? It is seldom less than three feet and probably not more than five – and a brooklet would be narrower; but a brook or a brooklet has to be crossed when it runs through the middle of the garden; and a bridge is usually provided for this purpose.

No doubt most people would employ a builder to erect one, especially if an arched one built of stone is wanted. Many gardeners, however, are handymen and quite capable of building a simple wooden bridge. It would be no more difficult than building a pergola and it probably wouldn't take as long.

The site is important. The banks must be high enough, two feet being the minimum for a straight, wooden bridge – three feet would be ideal. Stone-work can of course be used to give additional height and will at the same time provide a good solid foundation for the structure.

The wood must be durable, such as oak or elm, at least for the foot-way; the sides, horizontals and uprights, are often made of larch-poles, however, and fashioned in the style of trellis-work used for rambler-roses.

Where there is a larger wooden bridge crossing a widish stream, the former can be used to support some flowering creeper like the Wisteria, which needs a deep, moist root-run if it is to flourish and flower profusely. In Monet's garden at Giverny (see page 54), a bridge which crosses the Water-lily pool has Wisteria trained over it; the long, pale purple flower-clusters are reflected in the water below, where pink and scarlet Water-lilies grow.

Wisteria is too large a plant, however, for the small narrow bridges that most of us will want to build.

Stepping-stones are often used instead of a bridge for crossing shallow water; I say shallow advisedly, since it is unwise to use them, even if they can be obtained big enough, in a deep, fast-flowing stream; and they look most appropriate in a stream or brook that runs through a wild type of garden.

They are occasionally seen in wild parts of a garden, set among grass in shady places, where they give one the impression that the ground is damp or swampy. (Similarly in Japanese gardens stones are embedded at intervals in a bed of sand to suggest a running stream; overhanging trees like Willows enhance the illusion – see page 15.)

On the wet ground of a Bog-garden they are essential and should have reasonably level and fairly smooth tops that are comfortable to stand on; and they should be big enough to take a good-sized foot. If they are too small and irregularly shaped (say, slightly pointed) and also too widely spaced, they can cause a person to overbalance, which is perhaps of little moment when he is crossing a Bog-garden but unpleasant in the middle of a stream.

Grey, weathered stone gives a cooler effect in grass or in the wild-garden than reddish or buff-coloured sandstone; but for a brook either is suitable; and both can be obtained from any landscape nurseries. Half a dozen would be enough for a widish brook; personally I prefer to have a double row: the second lot set 18 inches or so away from the first, the stones being alternately placed instead of opposite.

It is possible to make one's own stepping-stones cheaply from cement and sand, a reliable mixture consisting of one part cement and three parts sand. Normally it is necessary to have a wooden mould in which to shape the cement, but with stepping-stones, holes made in the ground are as good. I make mine 14 inches deep by 12 inches wide. It is an easy matter to shape the tops nice and level. The sides of the holes should be lined with stiff brown paper or with cardboard to facilitate the removal of the stepping-stones when the cement has firmly set. Leave it in the holes for a week.

It shouldn't be a difficult job to set them in position in the Bog-garden; if the soil is exceptionally oozy, remove sufficient of the mud to enable you to make a good foundation with rubble or flints, etc. (It is not a difficult job to make a small Bog-garden by using a cement tray-like foundation, or basin, to hold the wet peaty soil; constructional hints are given in chapter 9.)

Positioning the stones in a brook is more troublesome; various

methods have been used: from damming up the stream to divert-
ing it temporarily into a canal specially made by the side of it
– both quite lengthy jobs.

I think it more simple to wait first till mid-summer or till such
a time when the water is at its lowest point. During a drought
the bed of a shallow stream may become reasonably dry, or dry
enough, to enable one to dig out foundation holes for the stones,
which must be placed very firmly in position.

Failing this, however, there is a simple method of damming or
control: sharply-pointed strips of wood or metal (about 6 inches
wide and 2 feet high – the height depending on the depth of the
water) are driven into the bed of the stream close together to
form two L-shaped structures, the base of each L beginning at
the bank, close enough to prevent much water seeping through;
the uprights coming parallel in the middle of the stream. (See
Fig. 1.) This wooden structure will force most of the water
through the narrow channel formed by the uprights and keep
the water low enough by the banks to enable one to fix the
stones in position. This method of damming can of course only
be attempted in a shallow stream. Sunk 3 or 4 inches into the
stream-bed, the stones will be firmly positioned and secure.

Artificial cascades were among the favourite water devices
which featured in many of the famous old Italian gardens.
Natural cascades are rare, except in streams which flow rapidly
through mountainous country. In a garden stream they can be
suggested by the simple method of placing large pieces of rock
at intervals along the stream-bed, which will cause the water to
swirl round and eddy about before it flows smoothly on again.

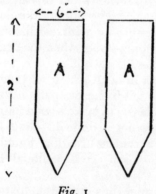

Fig. 1

And where there is a shallow stream with high banks, blocks of stone can be piled up in the water to make a sort of dam to hold it back temporarily and force it upwards; it will then gush over

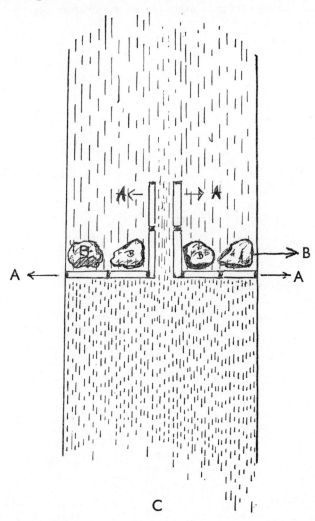

Fig. 2

A = sharply-pointed sections of wood or metal
B = stepping-stones
C = plan of stream showing position of strips of wood forming L-shaped structure to control flow of water

the top and form quite a realistic cascade. It is now possible, however, to buy specially-constructed cascade-pools with an electric pump to control the flow of water which is forced upwards from a bottom supply pool. (See chapter 10, pages 140 and 141.)

CHAPTER TWO

Riverside Gardens

SPRINGS AND BOGS

RIVERSIDE gardens are rare. Very few houses are built close enough to a river for their owners to enjoy a water frontage. Usually a towing-path or a public footpath runs along the banks and the houses stand some distance back – perhaps a quarter of a mile away.

Now and then, however, houses have a private river frontage (especially those in a riverside town or village), the gardens extending to the water-edge. It sounds exciting. Often though the bank is high, the water flowing a foot or two below. In that case it is of no practical garden value – the roots of many moisture-loving plants, such as the Bog Primulas, cannot get down to it. On the other hand, moisture-loving trees and shrubs, Willows, for instance, are well suited here.

More often than not the chief concern of the owner of such a garden is to have a suitable landing-stage for boats. This means that steps of some sort, usually of stone, must be set in the bank as a landing-stairs, to enable people to reach the garden from the river.

The low bank, or the gentle slope from the water-edge, or a bay-like opening, is more easily planted. On a low bank moisture-loving plants may be grown. Many Primulas flourish luxuriantly near water – many *in* water – and there are dozens of other things.

What could be lovelier than the old-fashioned, well-known 'Pheasant-Eye' Narcissus massed on a river bank, quite close to the edge (it is excellent for naturalizing in moist places); it has pure white slightly reflexed petals and a yellow eye edged with crimson; and the flowers are delightfully fragrant.

The Trumpet Daffodils prefer moist situations and shady places – plant them under the spreading branches of some tree which likes a damp spot – such as Willows (*Salix*); Alders

39

(*Alnus*); Birches (*Betula*). A fine Daffodil for naturalizing is 'King Alfred,' with rich golden-yellow trumpets on extra long stems.

Plant Bluebells, Hyacinths and some of the long-stemmed Tulips; the last two will need lifting when they have finished flowering; but the Bluebells and the Narcissi may be left undisturbed for many years. (Leave them permanently if you like.)

Most hardy bulbs thrive in moist situations and many can be naturalized in grass. On the bank of a river, especially the low bank, which may be flooded in winter, they are best grown this way: remove some of the turf, make a suitable place for them and then replace the turf, rolling it lightly (or treading it) in position. Safe (more or less) under the grass, they are not likely to be disturbed by swiftly-moving flood water. In open soil they are soon swept away. And this of course is the fate of all shallow-rooting plants. Deep rooting things like Bamboos and most trees and shrubs are safe, unless the flood water is exceptionally deep and swift – in that case everything goes. Needless to say, all newly-planted trees should be very firmly staked and the stakes renewed when they show any signs of rotting.

The hybrid Laburnum, *L.* × *vossii*, with very long hanging racemes of golden-yellow flowers, is sometimes planted near the edge of a river, and when the tree isn't staked, or when the stakes have been removed – perhaps after some years – it begins to slant forward and in a short time will be growing at an angle instead of upright. Finally it will fall. This happens to many trees and shrubs whose roots lie near the surface. They are not suitable for riverside planting. (Personally I'd never plant anything of much value on a river bank, apart from Willows, if I knew there was a risk of flooding.)

Where the water near the bank is shallow, many of the water-loving Irises such as the Sibiricas may be grown. Don't attempt any such planting if the water is high, but wait till it drops. It can be done any time through the summer.

Set these tall Sibirica Irises in clay in the water, keeping the clay firmly round the fibrous roots with heavy stones or rocks. The roots must be set close against the river bank. You will find that in a season or two the Irises will have become firmly established.

All Irises, ornamental Rushes and similar plants when grown

in running water should be secured in some such way as this. And the best time for the work naturally is mid-summer, when the river level is low. Many gardeners use tubs or wire baskets such as those used for planting Water-lilies; but baskets are difficult to secure to a bank and should be kept for Water-lilies which are to be grown in still water.

Another method, one I have used successfully on a low bank, is to remove some of the soil from the base, which isn't difficult to reach when the water is low, and insert the Iris or Rush, or whatever you want to grow, in the cavity. Loosen as much of the soil as you can and keep the plant in position with a large stone or a piece of rock placed in front of it. Most plants are sent out nowadays in containers (flower-pot-shaped) made of a paper-like substance which soon rots away when left in earth or water.

Our two native Irises, the Yellow Flag (*Iris pseudacorus*) and the Gladwyn Iris, lilac-blue (both described in the previous chapter, page 29) are best grown in shallow water. Fix them in clay close against the river-bank. The latter plant is only 2 feet tall and hardly suitable perhaps for the riverside.

Don't attempt to grow any of the glorious 'Clematis Irises' (*Iris kaempferi*): they are too precious to risk in flowing water. Furthermore, they are too dwarf for many rivers and need rampantly fertile soil – rich, deep loam consisting of sifted peat or leafmould, coarse sand and heavy fibrous loam; they should also be fed regularly with liquid manure through the growing season. Plant them in shallow artificial pools or ponds or canals, where the water is easily controlled. (See chapter 1, page 30 for lists of varieties.)

Ornamental Reeds and Rushes such as the Bulrush and the Reed Mace (both natives of Britain) are best grown in the water, close to the bank. The Bulrush is *not* the tall Reed with the cylindrical brown spike; the correct popular name of this plant is the Reed Mace. (Mace probably refers to the spike or truncheon-like shape of the inflorescence.) Its specific name is *Typha latifolia*. It often reaches a height of 8 feet and is too big and too rampant for a stream or a small pool. The leaves are long, narrow and smooth; the brown spikes stand up well above them and are often used for indoor decoration during the winter. Set the rhizome an inch or two deep in the soil (in about a foot of water near the bank). The plant will require no further

B*

attention, unless it spreads too far; in that case the rhizomes should be cut away with a sharp-edged spade.

The Bulrush is a less interesting plant, I think. Bulrush is a corruption of Pool Rush, by which popular name the plant was known: more often than not it is called Club Grass or Club Rush. Its specific name is *Scirpus lacustris*. It is usually about 8 feet tall. The stems are roundish and the flowers (grass-like and inconspicuous) come at the tips. Set the roots in the bed of the river (in shallow water); a large stone will keep the plant firmly in place. See Fig. 3, a, b, c, page 52. (These two Rushes can be bought from any nursery and cost about 3s. each.)

Bamboos are fine plants for the riverside garden, provided the district is warm enough for them, and a spot sheltered from cold biting winds can be found. Unfortunately there is nearly always a wind blowing up the river, which isn't good for most of these plants.

But the hardiest and toughest of them will thrive on many river banks. *Arundinaria anceps* is one: a tall Bamboo from the Himalayas, with stems up to 14 feet high and arching at the top. They are from $\frac{1}{4}$ inch to $\frac{1}{2}$ inch thick, purplish at first, then changing to brownish-green. The narrow leaves (the longest 4 inches long and $\frac{1}{2}$ inch wide) are a brilliant green above and glaucous beneath. This Bamboo does best on a river-bank facing south, in a warm, sheltered situation; it spreads rapidly by its underground stems. On a low bank it could be controlled by sinking corrugated iron round it; this would probably drive some of the underground stems down into the river, but it would be very effective there and in clear, shallow water would flourish and eventually make a charming edging of arching canes and foliage.

One of the tallest and most imposing of the hardy Bamboos is *A. fastuosa*; its canes go up to a height of 20 feet or more and carry dark, lustrous green leaves (the largest 8 inches long by 1 inch wide). It is less rampant than some of the other *Arundinaria*: an ideally graceful plant for a river-bank. (Plant it fairly well back: too near the edge, it is often battered about by wind and damaged.)

A. japonica (12 feet) and *A. palmata* (8 feet) are two other hardy species I recommend.

Another group of Bamboos are the *Phyllostachys*, which are frequently grown on river-banks. There is a very tall one, viz. *Phyllostachys viridi-glaucescens*, whose stems arch outwards and will touch the water; and a dwarf one – *P. ruscifolia*, 2 feet high, which makes a charming clump of slender canes (⅛th of an inch thick) carrying dark glossy green foliage.

There are several other species of Bamboos offered by nurseries. But before ordering any, it would be wise to find out which are the most suitable kinds for the district where they are to be grown. They are expensive plants to buy, and some are suitable only for the warmest gardens in our southernmost counties.

Finding the right place for them in small riverside gardens is sometimes difficult; only one variety should be grown and a moderate-sized one or a dwarf should be chosen. In these small gardens, which are often bounded by division walls or hedges, the best place for a moderate-sized Bamboo is against one of the boundaries. A clump near the river, with a stone background or a clipped hedge, is most effective.

The very tall varieties are quite out of place and look odd planted on a small river frontage. On a long bank, however, and standing well back, the 20-foot tall *Phyllostachys viridi-glaucescens* grown as a specimen clump is magnificent. Its spreading roots may in time invade the grass pathway or the verge; and they should be hacked away or dug out with a pick-axe or a very sharp spade.

What should be grown with Bamboos? They are unique plants and it is difficult to find anything suitable to go with them. Perhaps some of the taller hardy Ferns, such as the Broad Buckler Fern (*Dryopteris dilatata*), would be the best choice. Flowers should not be used – even the tall *Iris sibirica* produces an incongruous effect. In big riverside gardens I have seen them grown near a Weeping Willow, the Willow near enough to the bank for its long hanging branches to be touching the water, and clumps of tall Bamboos standing a little distance back from the tree. The sharp contrast was not altogether pleasing. I have also seen some of the taller Bamboos planted behind Yuccas (evergreen plants with rosettes of narrow, usually rigid leaves); this association was excellent and particularly attractive on a sloping river-bank.

Willows are by far the best things for growing near the riverside. As I've already mentioned (page 21), the tree kinds are too large when fully grown for streams and small artificial pools.

Salix alba is the native White Willow, a tall tree with branches pendulous at the ends and carrying leaves covered with a silky grey down, which gives them a whitish appearance. It is not as striking though as the variety SERICEA, which has leaves of a silvery hue; this becomes a shining white when seen from a distance. Like the Weeping Willow (*S. babylonica*), it is best grown as a single specimen.

S. × *salamonii* is a fine riverside Willow. It is a hybrid between *S. alba* and *S. babylonica*; a vigorous tall tree (up to 60 feet in height) and hardier than *S. babylonica*, though not so elegant in form, being of more upright habit. The narrow leaves are green above and of a bluish-white hue beneath. It is more of a success in cold districts than the Weeping Willow. It can be planted in shallow water near the river-bank in mid-summer, when the water is reasonably low. The soil can be more easily removed then; place the tree in position and cover the roots with some heavy loam – it can be pressed firmly round them with your hands or with the handle of a garden-fork. Tie the tree very securely to a strong stake set well down in the river-bank.

These Willows are among the most striking for specimen planting on the bank of a large riverside garden; as I've already mentioned, they are too big for limited spaces and in time would completely cover an artificial pool. (They can be obtained from any good shrub nursery and cost about 10s. 6d. each.)

The smaller trees, bushes and dwarf species are well suited to narrower streams, pools and ponds, the tiny alpine ones (only a few inches high) making admirable foliage plants for the rockery and for rockery pools.

In winter I like to see clumps of the species noted for the brilliant colour of their stems planted on a river bank. These Willows are pollarded or cut back regularly as a rule (about every second spring) to produce wands or erect slender stems. If they are to be grown primarily for decorative effect in winter, they are best cut down to ground level, so that dense clumps or thickets are obtained. The massed red, yellow, and purple cane-like growths are uncommonly beautiful seen in winter sunshine against the river flowing by. *Salix vitellina* Var. BRITZENSIS is the reddish-stemmed Willow and will shine a brilliant scarlet in the winter sun. The species *S. vitellina* is a warm golden-yellow; and *S. daphnoides* a purple-violet with a blue-white bloom. (The smallest specimens cost about 12s. 6d. each, according to 1967 price lists.)

The Weeping Willow is incomparably the best tree for planting on a river-bank, high or low; but it should not be grown actually in the river, since the great charm of the tree lies in its long hanging branches reaching over and touching the surface of the water.

Alders (*Alnus*) are perhaps the toughest and strongest of all riverside trees: suitable for high or low banks or for growing in the water. But they are nowhere near as attractive as the Willows. (Indeed, they are disliked by many people.) The Common Alder (*Alnus glutinosa*) can spring up anywhere, in any garden, as a seedling shrub; and it ultimately makes a tall tree, 80 or 90 feet in height. It hasn't much to recommend it, though, as a garden tree; and anybody wanting an Alder for riverside planting should choose the variety IMPERIALIS, which has finely cut leaves and is consequently much more ornamental than the type plant (species). The astonishing thing is that the species is to be found listed in so many shrub catalogues. It is one of our most common wildings and scarcely worth the half a guinea asked for it.

A better garden tree is *A. incana*, a native of Europe and the Caucasus, but not of Britain. Its popular name is the Grey Alder; and the plant has ovalish leaves, dull green above and grey beneath. It is very hardy and in the coldest, wet soil will make a fine tree 70 feet tall with a trunk 6 feet in girth. I prefer the varieties, however, for growing on the bank of a riverside garden. And the handsomest is Var. LACINIATA (ACUMINATA), which was awarded a First Class Certificate in 1873. The leaves are beautifully dissected, being divided into 6 or 8 pairs of narrow, toothed lobes. It is quite expensive to buy and a few years ago cost about a guinea.

I recommend Var. AUREA, too, with its young shoots and foliage, a charming golden yellow all through the summer and its catkins a conspicuous red colour.

Other Alders suitable for planting near or in water are *Alnus nitida*, known as the Himalayan Alder (up to 50 feet high in cultivation), and *A. rugosa* (*serrulata*), the Smooth Alder – not particularly ornamental but ideal for wet, cold soils.

There are several trees and shrubs commonly called 'Swamp' plants; but not all of them flourish in swamps. The Swamp

Cypress, a deciduous conifer is, however, a genuine waterside plant, and flourishes in boggy places. *Taxodium distichum* is its specific name; it is a native of the South-eastern States of the U.S.A. and is found copiously in the low swampy ground round the Gulf of Mexico. It should whenever possible be planted on a mound or in some raised soil in the water, as it is in the Lily Pond at Kew Botanic Gardens. The immersed part of the trunk becomes swollen and spongy, but above the water line the tree soars up often to a height of 100 feet or more. Its soft yellow-green foliage in early spring is an enchantment, and it has a second season of loveliness in Autumn.

Glyptostrobus pensilis is another Swamp Cypress (the Chinese Swamp Cypress) but more tender than the *Taxodium*, to which it is related. It has leaves a charming soft green which tint beautifully, like those of the other tree before they fall. The plant has been tried in sheltered gardens near London (planted near a warm wall), but was a failure there. It is indubitably a moisture-loving shrub for warm, swampy situations in our southernmost sheltered gardens. Its charming autumn foliage makes it an exquisite pot plant; and many people grow the plant in a cool greenhouse and use it for indoor decoration.

Several Poplars thrive in wet, heavy ground (particularly the so-called Black Poplars), but as they are surface-rooting and grow rapidly, they are suitable only for isolated places in the very biggest gardens. One often sees them lining avenues or bordering towing paths. The hybrid forms are more frequently grown now than *Populus nigra*, called the true Black Poplar.

One of the finest is *P.* × *serotina* Var. AUREA, a tall tree 100 feet or more in height, with pure yellow leaves in spring and early summer, which turn yellow-green later. In fact the tree is known as the Golden Poplar.

Some gardeners give *Populus heterophylla* as a suitable species for waterside planting. In its habitat it makes a tall tree up to 100 feet, with astonishingly large leaves, heart-shaped and 7 or 8 inches long and wide, first covered with a thick, whitish down then ultimately dark green. It is an American species (from the eastern States); but by no means a good grower in Britain, actually it is never more than a shrub about 5 feet in height. Its popular name is the Swamp Cottonwood, which suggests that it is suitable for riverside planting. (The name 'Swamp' is sometimes misleading, however: the Swamp Honeysuckle, *Rhodo-*

dendron viscosum, for instance, doesn't flourish in wet soils. It likes plenty of moisture, but won't tolerate stagnant moisture round its roots.)

For my part, I would never grow any flowering shrubs on a riverbank where there was a risk of flooding. Dwarf Rhododendrons massed near the river are a magnificent sight, but they are easily uprooted by deep swirling water.

As regards the slope up from the water edge or the bay-like opening in the riverbank (mentioned at the beginning of the chapter – see page 39), this would probably be used as a landing place for boats, rather like a 'beach,' and doubtless few people would want to grow anything on it.

A gradual slope up from the water (or an opening in the bank) is very useful and not difficult to make when the bank is low. Simply remove sufficient soil to level the bank to the water edge. (It would be necessary in most localities to obtain permission from the River Commissioners or the River Conservancy to do this.) There is no danger of any flooding, since the water near the bank is shallow and flows past with the main stream. Only during exceptionally wet winters would it rise high enough to cover the slope completely. Those who want to plant it, would have to consider this contingency when deciding what to grow. It would be wisest to choose things that are inexpensive – especially those that can be raised from seed. You can get seeds of most Bog Primulas and many water-loving Irises such as the Sibiricas. The varieties EMPEROR; PERRY'S BLUE; and LAVENDER I have raised from 1s. packets of seed. Some of the tall Candelabra or Asiatic Primulas are ideal for planting on a riverside slope. (See chapter 1, page 25, *et seq.* where different kinds are described.) These will grow and flourish in shallow water; but expensive varieties should not be bought, since in all probability they will be under water during the winter months and will ultimately perish. They are all right at the edge of a shallow stream, or *in* the stream; but they will not survive many seasons at the edge of a river. It is wise to sow seeds of these plants every spring so as to have a good stock in hand to replace casualties.

I think a paved pathway down to the water's edge is an excellent idea; first, it breaks up the area of the slope, preventing it from looking like a flower patch when all the Primulas are in bloom; and secondly, the pathway can be used for approaching the water for the purpose of getting into a boat.

Paving-stones or flagstones can usually be bought at a builder's yard; or you can make good imitation ones with cement and sand – they should be fairly thick (not less than an inch) and about 18 inches square. And the pathway should be fairly wide: 4 feet is ideal; though the width will depend on the size of the slope. The pathway could commence well back in the garden and lead down to the river, the last flagstones being half in the water. They should all be well embedded in cement on a good, solid foundation.

SPRINGS AND BOGS

The definition of a spring is 'a flow of water rising or issuing naturally out of the earth.' It is the source of rivers and often comes from mountain slopes and hills. The Thames, for instance, is formed by head-streams which come from the south-eastern slopes of the Cotswold Hills. Springs may be seen in the Thames Valley trickling over fields not far from the river; and in some places the water has been diverted into beds or ditches and used for cultivating Water-cress. I imagine there are very few gardens though through which a spring flows.

The Savill Garden at Windsor (a vast natural woodland garden) is watered by rain-water springs which trickle over the grass and finally collect in a stream at the lowest part of the grounds.* At times, especially during a wet April, the water flows freely, and visitors have to pick their steps in the grass. The ground is spongy, often wet, but as the water on the slopes is never stagnant it has been possible to grow many charming moisture-loving plants there.

In February the grass is dotted about with tiny Daffodils (miniature Narcissi). Many of these are best naturalized as they are here, and left to spread and increase.

One of the best is *Narcissus bulbocodium*, the Hoop-Petticoat Daffodil with crinoline-shaped flowers and conspicuous anthers standing out from the tiny trumpets. There are white and yellow forms, and the plants are about 6 inches high. Other varieties are CITRINUS, with lemon-yellow flowers; GRAELLSII,

---

* Clay and the top soil (Bagshot sand) act as a reservoir and the water contained in the soil gradually seeps down to the lowest part of the garden.

primrose-yellow; MONOPHYLLUS, a pretty species with white flowers, a native of Algeria and Spain. *N. cyclamineus,* the Cyclamen-flowered Daffodil, is another charming little species for naturalizing in moist grassland. The flowers are drooping, frilled, and of a lemon-yellow colour; they bloom in February.

The new Var. PEEPING TOM is taller (up to 15 inches in height) and has narrow, golden-yellow trumpets. All these miniature Daffodils do best in a damp place. Ideally this is a sloping piece of grass land. They look natural there. They are too small to be grown among other plants, near streams or rivers.

Our native Wood Anemone, *Anemone nemorosa,* with its modest, white flowers which come in March, is a good plant to grow with miniature Daffodils – there are plenty of these that bloom at the same time as the Anemone. And of course in a big woodland garden wild flowers spring up, many quite charming, such as the pale mauve Milk Maids (*Cardamine pratensis*); Ragged Robin; the purple Marsh Orchis (*Orchis latifolia*); but often Daisies, Buttercups, Dandelions and the like are the strongest growers. Owners of a wild garden get rid of these weeds as soon as they appear; for if they are left more than a season they soon spread and overrun the choicer things.

As already mentioned, Water-cress is cultivated in gardens where a natural spring flows, though very few people would go to the trouble of growing it; most of our Watercress comes from nurseries and small holders who are able to grow large quantities for the market.

The plant is *Nasturtium officinale,* with small divided leaves, green or brownish in colour, and terminal tufts of white flowers. The beds are usually 3 to 4 feet wide and about 6 inches deep; they can be any length, and spring water flows continuously through them.

A bog is best described as a piece of low-lying ground which is permanently wet or spongy and too soft to bear the weight of anything heavy on it; it consists usually of decayed mosses and vegetable matter. Only certain kinds of plants that will tolerate stagnant moisture will live in a bog – coarse grasses and mosses usually. There is nothing beautiful about a bog, then, and they are never found in gardens. They are desolate areas, uncultivated, barren and useless, except for those parts where there are thick peat formations, the peat being cut out and used as fuel as it is in certain parts of Ireland. The famous Bog of Allen is a

dreary expanse of peat east of the Shannon. The garden Bog is
of course an artificial feature and created expressly for the cultivation of attractive moisture-loving plants. (It is fully described
in chapter 9, page 118.) Nevertheless in a garden where there is
a stream running through it, or in a riverside garden, there are
frequently areas (perhaps quite small) near the water which are
swampy for most of the year.

Mimulus (Musk or Monkey Flowers) will thrive there, and
may live on through spells of very dry weather, provided they
are growing in a deep rich loam in a shady spot. *Mimulus luteus*,
a native of Chile, has become naturalized in Great Britain, and
is found at the edges of shallow streams and ditches. It has
bright yellow flowers and is about 2 feet tall. It increases rapidly
by means of its rooting stems and self-sown seeds. A finer garden
plant is the variety A. T. JOHNSON, whose flowers are heavily
spotted with red.

One can buy these plants for about half a crown each; and
they are easily raised from seed. And the seed may be broadcast
in April in the place near the stream or the pond where the
plants are to grow and flower.

Another shade-loving perennial for a swampy place is the
Scarlet Lychnis (*Lychnis chalcedonica*), with vivid blood-red
flower-heads in summer. It can be raised from seed in spring,
and the seedlings potted up and kept for planting out the following May. The Scarlet Lychnis (often grown in the herbaceous
border) is 3 feet tall; and its flowers stand out delightfully
against the fresh green foliage. To get the best effect, the plant
should be massed. The stems are usually cut down in the
autumn and they shoot up again in March. It is very hardy and
will probably live for a number of years in swampy ground.

Our common Purple Loosestrife or Willow-weed, *Lythrum
salicaria*, is a tough plant and beautiful in the mass.* It seems to
grow anywhere; this plant and its more attractive variety
BRIGHTNESS (a clear rose colour) do well in partial shade in
damp soils. The deep rose-pink PRITCHARD'S VARIETY; and THE
BEACON (deep crimson) give a fine show when massed. They
bloom in July and August and may be raised from seed.

Even if the ground by the stream or the river dries out during
a hot summer – and this often happens in the Thames Valley –

---

* It spreads too rapidly however and soon overruns choicer things. Useful
only in the largest gardens.

all these plants will survive if they have been planted in deep rich leafy soil and are protected from the sun.

Where the ground is constantly wet, as it is at the edge of a stream or a ditch watered by a natural spring, the early-blooming *Primula denticulata* may be grown. It is one of the most charming of the smaller kinds for a permanently damp situation. The plant has a long blooming season – from March till May. It forms close rosettes of leaves, narrow, toothed and crinkly; and from them spring up the stems 8 to 12 inches long, which carry globular heads of lilac-coloured flowers. Like many Primulas, it is essentially a plant for damp places where the water is clear and fresh. This lovely Primula and several of its varieties – the white ALBA and the deep red PRITCHARD'S RUBY – will be found near the stream at the Savill Gardens, Windsor.

It is a good plan to visit those gardens where water has been used in the lay-out of the grounds; in riverside gardens, for instance, it is interesting to see what has been made of the river frontage. And in many river districts one can take trips by steamer and view the gardens at leisure from the boat. Usually the first thing that attracts the eye is the well-kept grass – deep green, soft and well mown – which often extends from the house down to the water-edge. It is a feature in itself (cool and refreshing to see) and perhaps could not be improved upon. A Willow tree is often the only ornament.

In some of these gardens formal beds have been made, cut out in the lawns, near the river. Filled with scarlet Geraniums (Zonal Pelargoniums), they are a magnificent sight, especially when viewed from the river.

To see what has been done with springs and bogs, those who are able to, should visit the Savill Gardens. Here the water trickling over the grass is something every gardener has dreamed of. As much water as one wants! And always fresh and pure.

Rare moisture-loving plants flourish luxuriantly in different parts of the grounds, and the water they need flows near and is in constant supply.

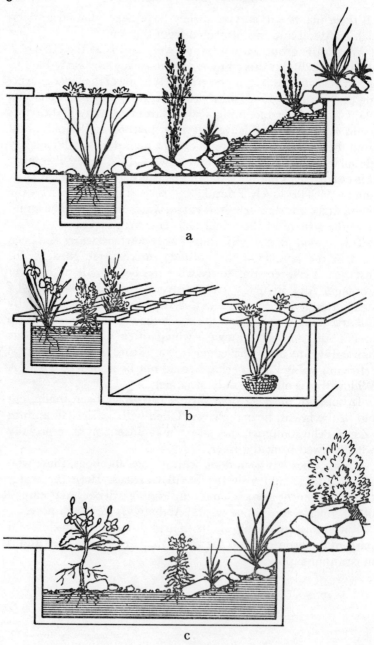

a

b

c

Fig. 3

CHAPTER THREE

Lakes, Ponds and Pools

A LAKE is a large mass of still water in a depression of the ground. The name is also applied to a widened part of a river; at Zürich, for instance, the lake (the Zürich See) is formed from the widened Limmat.

Natural lakes abound in Scotland and Ireland, but there are few in England; and when we mention 'lake' we usually think of the Lake District, which is one of the beauty spots of the country.

Lakeside gardens, like riverside gardens, are rare, but in Switzerland and Italy, where there are many vast lakes, towns and villages have sprung up round the shores and gardens sweep down to the water edge. They might be riverside gardens so far as expanse of water is concerned. There is little flooding, however, and consequently little erosion or wearing away of the soil of the banks. (It is worth mentioning here that with our modern methods of dredging and water control, riverbanks are safer. In the past not many riverside gardens escaped damage. And usually only Rushes and similarly tough aquatics which formed thick matted roots were grown along a riverbank. Trees were sometimes swept away during bad floods; or much of the soil from between their wide-spaced roots was washed into the river.)

A lake, correctly speaking, is sufficiently large to form a geographical feature; and the so-called garden lake is perforce an artificial one, big enough to sail a boat on or to fish in, perhaps; and sometimes very large, such as Hamilton's lake covering 30 acres, at Painshill, Cobham, Surrey, which he designed about the middle of the 18th century, a time when that most controversial figure in the world of landscape gardening, 'Capability' Brown was working. It was Brown who designed the great park at Blenheim, Oxfordshire, and dammed a stream to make the enormous lakes there. His work came in for much criticism,

53

however, from many of his contemporaries and those who followed him. Repton, in his book on landscape gardening (1806) mentions his dislike of Brown's use of water on hills. He says: 'in many places under his direction I have found water on the tops of hills, which I have been obliged to remove into lower ground, because the deception was not sufficiently complete to satisfy the mind as well as the eye.'

In most gardens lakes are built at ground level; and by a river this is necessary when the supply of water comes from the river, as it does at Kew Botanical Gardens. The lake there is a good-sized sheet of water, covering an area of about four and a half acres and is connected by an underground culvert or channel with the Thames, about 100 yards away. The banks are planted with Willows, Alders, Purple Loosestrife and many of the moisture-loving flowers I have mentioned that are suitable for riverside gardens and bogs.

Large lakes (covering acres of ground) are no longer made – in the average modern garden there wouldn't be room, anyway – instead we have pools or ornamental ponds, which are designed chiefly for growing the most attractive of all aquatics, viz., the hardy Water-lilies (*Nymphaea*).

Every gardener of my acquaintance nowadays wants a Lily-pool with goldfish in it; and they are right to consider such a feature as one that gives more pleasure perhaps than any other. It has life, movement, and reflects light and colour.

Monet* saw that and planned a Lily Pool in his garden. In 1883 he bought a peasant's orchard at Giverny, near which flowed the Epte, a tributary of the Seine, and from this created his famous Water-garden. He was able to divert the stream and make a pool and grow in it the Nymphaeas which he painted towards the end of his life. In the book *À Giverny, chez Claude Monet* he says: 'It took me a long time to understand my Water-lilies and I tended them without any thought of painting them.'

Later he enlarged the pool, extending it at one end and narrowing it so that he could build a wooden bridge across the water. Sluice-gates at each end controlled the flow of water to and from the stream. He planted not only Water-lilies but Irises, Weeping Willows and Bamboos on the banks, and Wis-

* Claude Monet, Impressionist painter, born in Paris 1840, died at Giverny in 1926.

teria on the bridge to drip over the side and appear mirrored in the water; and he used Rambler Roses for a background.

There couldn't be a better place for training Wisteria than on a wooden bridge over a stream or a pool, as it is done at Giverny. This climber, of which there are several species and varieties, needs full sun on its flowering stems (which it gets when exposed on a bridge), and moisture at its roots, which is always plentiful in the soil near a pool or a stream. Wisterias won't thrive in shallow, chalky soils and will never flower in shady places.

The finest in my opinion is *Wisteria floribunda* var. MACRO-BOTRYS, with exceptionally long racemes – sometimes 3 feet or more in length. It is widely cultivated in Japan (is actually known as the Japanese Wisteria) and the variety depicted in their decorative paintings and prints. The flowers, purplish or purplish-violet, are fragrant and come in racemes (usually very long) and about 3 inches wide. The leaves are a dark glossy green and the twining branches will reach a height of 30 feet or more. It blooms in May as a rule and is a hardier plant than the better known *W. sinensis*. *W. floribunda* and its varieties (there are four in cultivation) are natives of Japan, but only the type plant (the species) has been found genuinely wild.

I have seen Var. MACROBOTRYS growing up trees, but much of its beauty was lost: the long hanging flowers don't show up to best advantage among the branches and dense foliage of a tree. This plant is best on a pergola or trained along the wooden railings of a bridge over a stream. Wooden supports are much better for the plant than iron, which tends to get hot when exposed for a long period to the sun. And the beauty of the flowers is enhanced by reflection.

I have not seen Var. ROSEA, with pale rose-coloured flowers; but I know Var. ALBA, with rather shorter racemes, white tinged with delicate lilac. A lovely plant.

W. sinensis, a native of China, is the species most commonly grown in our gardens. It has fragrant lilac flowers carried in racemes usually about a foot long; its leaves are a deep rich green; and the plant will grow very tall on trees and any similar vertical support. It best displays its charming hanging flowers, however, when it is trained horizontally on a pergola or on a wall. It will be necessary at times to cut out some of the growths and crowded stems when they make too thick a tangle. (More information about the cultivation of Wisteria will be found in chapter 13.)

Rambler Roses and Weeping Willows were used by Monet as background plants. Ramblers are well suited to some sort of formal planting as, for instance, near a pond or a pool which has its sides faced with brick, the roses trailing in festoons over the edge down to the water. This is how they are grown near the pond at Kew.

The Irises Monet grew were used as models for his painting *Irises in The Water-Garden, Giverny*. In the picture they seem to be growing in the water. Actually they are planted at the edge of the pool. A frequent visitor to Giverny during Monet's time informs me that they were specimens of the common blue-mauve *germanica* Irises and were planted in heavy loam with an admixture of lime-rubble. Water-lilies floated on the water behind them.*

The Water-lilies, which served as models for Monet's paintings were some of the Marliac hybrids raised by M. Bory Latour-Marliac at his gardens near Temple-sur-Lot, in the South of France.

The first that Marliac produced was the lovely *Nymphaea* × *marliacea* Var. ROSEA; it appeared in 1879 and has extra large rose and white flowers, which are delightfully fragrant, and magnificent deep green leaves.

Monet's Nymphaeas were mostly pink or rose, and yellow varieties. Two of the finest are *N.* × *marliacea* Var. RUBRA PUNCTATA (raised in 1889); it has globular medium-sized flowers of a deep rose colour and is suitable for large pools. And Var. CHROMATELLA is the yellow one: a charming canary-yellow Water-lily with deep yellow stamens and olive-green leaves mottled with bronze. Other hardy varieties are described in the following chapter, where hints on their cultivation are also given.

Both varieties described above are suitable for medium-sized

---

* Water-lilies form a background in the picture and are floating patterns reflecting light – light was the chief subject of late Impressionist painting. There is a wonderful sense of freedom and movement in this picture – one feels Monet was painting, as his friends often described him: *ainsi que l'oiseau chante* (as a bird sings).

The picture was completed about 1912 and is now in the possession of Mme. Katia Granoff, Paris.

pools. There are stronger-growing kinds for deep lakes; and some will thrive and bloom in rivers, if the water doesn't flow fast. Our native *N. alba* does well in streams as deep as 10 feet. Its white flowers are 4 to 6 inches across and its foliage deep green. It can be seen in certain parts of the Thames, in the reaches of the river above Marlow, for example, where it grows near the bank, and is probably kept stationary by the thick water-weeds, through which it thrusts its stems to the surface.

I give a list here of a few varieties which are suitable for growing in large lakes and deep water; I don't advocate growing them in streams or rivers, since Water-lilies are essentially plants for still, sunny waters. Most of them grow into large masses of leaves and flowers, covering perhaps a surface 8 square feet or more. They are normally planted in water from $2\frac{1}{2}$ to 3 feet deep.

Nymphaea alba Var. RUBRA needs, first and foremost, really cold water to grow in, if it is to thrive and bloom freely. Like all the red varieties, its colour is pale at first (soft pink), and then deepens to a rich red shade with maturity. This lovely, rarely-seen Water-lily was introduced by Froebel of Zürich in 1878. It is more commonly grown and does better in the colder lakes of Switzerland, which are fed by the snows of the Alps. It flourishes and flowers very freely too in the lakes and pools of Scandinavia. (It is commonly known as the Swedish Red Water lily.)

COL. A. J. WELCH (raised by Marliac). It has been called the easiest variety to grow, but according to some gardeners, produces too much foliage and is therefore not a satisfactory plant for garden lakes. I like it for its habit of flowering its deep yellow blooms six inches or so out of the water. It is the easiest of the hardy Water-lilies to transplant.

COLOSSEA (Marliac) is one of the finest for garden lakes, with enormous vermilion-crimson blooms. (It costs about 25s. a root, by the way, but is well worth it.)

GLADSTONIANA (produced by Richardson's nursery, Ohio, U.S.A.). This is considered to be the largest of all the white Water-lilies – the flowers frequently measure 8 inches across. They are delightfully fragrant, snow-white in colour, with golden-yellow stamens. The plant grows very big (it is ideally suited in a lake) and needs plenty of good deep loam to grow in.

GOLIATH (Marliac) has large tulip-shaped flowers with extra long petals, white tinged with rose. The white stamens and reddish-orange petaloids (small central petals) enhance the beauty of the colouring.

HEVER WHITE (raised by Astors). It has large milky-white star-shaped blooms floating on lovely green foliage. Unfortunately this variety doesn't flower freely in our colder districts. It needs plenty of room and is best in large, still, sunny lakes in the south.

LUSITANIA (a choice Marliac hybrid). This Water-lily carries deep rose flowers with a centre of conspicuous rich brown-red stamens; the leaves are touched with purple when young and turn deep green in the summer.

N. odorata GIGANTEA (known also as Var. HOPATCONG). A variety which grows in the south-eastern United States. It has very large pure white flowers and deep green leaves, and must be planted in a lake where the water is deep. It grows much too large for the average garden pool.

PICCIOLA (Marliac). Another huge flower – often 10 inches across; incongruous even in a moderately large pool (the plant would completely cover a small one in a short time). It grows strongly and carries masses of lovely crimson blooms. A beautiful plant for the middle of a lake.

N. tuberosa Var. PAESLINGBERG was raised in Austria and has very large pure white, cup-shaped fragrant flowers. Suitable only for a lake.

N. tuberosa Var. RICHARDSONI (raised by Richardson's) is also pure white in colour, the flowers globular in shape, with attractive green sepals. The plant is a strong grower and needs plenty of room.

VERA LOUISE has enormous soft rose-coloured flowers, which contrast beautifully with the deep green foliage. (The plant is said to be a cross between Var. GLADSTONIANA and Var. MARLIACEA ROSEA). A lovely mass of floating pink and green for a garden lake.

These dozen Water-lilies are the best of the largest varieties for growing in lakes. They are fairly expensive: roots cost about 25s. each.

Ponds and pools are common features of many parts of the country. They are often found by the side of a road, and some dry up during a long hot summer. They are not as a rule particularly attractive and not very clean-looking, being usually supplied by water that drains through from nearby fields, or runs off the roads. Although the water isn't clean in many of our so-called 'horse-ponds,' it is apparently good enough for animals to drink.

When these ponds have been neglected, they soon fill up with weeds and Rushes and in time most of the water is absorbed. Eventually they become swamps,* and the breeding place of frogs and flies. 'Pools mar all,' Francis Bacon wrote (1625), 'and make the garden unwholesome and full of flies and frogs.'

Stagnant water, especially a small expanse exposed to the sun all day, certainly attracts them. But often pools and lakes benefit from the presence of frogs, since the tadpoles hatched from their spawn live on algae which may spread and cover the water; therefore they do help to keep the water pure. They clear it and make it more healthy for many of the aquatics we want to grow.

I know of several roadside pools which were taken over by the owners of the adjoining land. One, with overhanging trees, was left practically wild and unattended, and during hot summers nearly always dried up. It was left untouched because nightin-gales used to sing there. These birds are attracted by water and build their nests near it.

Another pool was emptied during a dry summer, ladles and buckets being used to scoop out the thick muddy water. The soil at the bottom was clayey and impermeable; but more clay was added and puddled to make a good solid base. The depression was then filled with fresh water from the kitchen tap, a long hose being used for the purpose; and in the autumn it was stocked with fish and plants.

The wild Thorn bushes and a wild Cherry tree growing on the roadside on the outside of the pool were left, since they provided a good screen and helped to guard the privacy of the garden. At the back of the pool adjoining the roadside the Rose Bay or French Willow (*Epilobium angustifolium*), was planted. It is a weed 3 to 6 feet tall, with rose-coloured flowers in long terminal racemes. It spreads rapidly but is lovely in the mass (Monet grew it in his garden at Giverny). This lovely weed spread out into the Thorn bushes and round the Cherry tree.

The wild shrubs and plants on the other side of the pool had been grubbed up so that one had access to it from the garden, and here was planted *Epilobium hirsutum*, another charming

* This is sometimes the fate of natural lakes: they dry up and become bogs.

native weed, with pale pink flowers, blooming in July. It thrives in moist places. All Rushes were grubbed up: a wise move, since they spread rapidly and would soon overrun anything else choicer planted at the edge of the water. Irises took their place.

In the pool were planted two Water-lilies: one, the yellow *Nuphar lutea*, a native, with small fragrant flowers and deep green leaves, 8 to 12 inches across; the other: the North American *Nymphaea odorata*, a lovely, fragrant Water-lily, with white flowers tinged with pink, which open in the morning and close at noon. A little large for the pool, which was only about 12 feet across; but the plant was kept within bounds by pruning it back with a pair of long-handled shears.

On the whole, these natural roadside pools are not very satisfactory as garden features; they usually collect a lot of sediment, washed in from the roads by heavy rains; consequently the water is often dirty and becomes polluted and destructive to plant and animal life. Artificial pools are often best built in the centre of the garden so that there is no danger of impurities from the road reaching the water. But one should never do away with a natural pool wherever it occurs, for it could be used as a sort of sump when draining water from an artificial pool, a canal or narrow channel being made to connect the two.

Natural waterfalls and cascades are practically non-existent in gardens. Cascades were mentioned briefly in chapter 1, page 36.

Artificial waterfalls are only possible in the largest gardens and there must be an abrupt declivity, or one must be made, over which the water can fall – those who garden on a hillside would probably have a suitable spot. But in the modern garden the miniature waterfall or a single drip of water is all that is wanted. It is often an integral part of a rockery, the water falling or dripping from a pool at the top into another at the bottom, usually a distance of about 6 feet. The water is sometimes supplied from a tap in the garden (the water having been laid on for that purpose) or special electrical apparatus to supply the motive power is installed as it is for an electrically-operated fountain. (See page 18 and chapter 10.)

Bacon, who didn't approve of ponds and pools in gardens, was enthusiastic about fountains: 'Fountains are a great beauty and refreshment.' They are not wanted, however, by owners of small gardens who grow Water-lilies and other aquatics which require still water. But it would be possible, of course, to have a fountain in a separate pool in another part of the garden.

An attractive feature – an original *motif* of a Water-garden – consists of two pools connected by a narrow canal or channel, both pools and canal being outlined or bordered by flagstones of an appropriate size, and the whole feature set in a fresh, green lawn. In the second pool, at the farthest end of the garden, a single jet is installed, the water rising 6 or 8 feet into the air and falling again into the stone basin or pool beneath. The water in the narrow canal connecting the two pools, is stationary, for small divisions of brick or cement at each end confine it. In the first, the nearer pool, grow the Water-lilies, and goldfish swim there among the leaves and the flowers which float on the still water. It is a feature which certainly provides beauty and refreshment.

The Japanese Garden introduced as a single feature needs a fairly large garden. Owners of small gardens sometimes convert them into Japanese Gardens, though it is easier to begin with a new plot – it is much less arduous. It is easier to plant afresh than to transplant; easier to design a new garden than to alter an old one. The Japanese Garden, a fascinating type of Water-garden, is described and discussed in chapter 11, page 144.

Finally, the Bathing-pool – today perhaps the most important piece of water in the garden! The plutocratic blue-tiled kinds, long and wide, with diving-boards, and set in the middle of a spacious lawn, we used to associate with film-stars and Hollywood. But now the cost of building one comes within the reach of many people, and it's not a difficult job to build one's own; there are exciting new ways of doing it and new and cheaper materials available. Bathing-pools can be made picturesque features of a garden. You can read about them further on in the book (page 96).

CHAPTER FOUR

Some Hardy Water-lilies

I⊤ is good to know something of the history of the plants we grow. About our loveliest Water-lilies, however, there isn't much to say; only the usual horticultural information is available; for they are all hybrids, and none was raised much before the last two decades of the 19th century. Horticultural information of the technical kind – such as that concerning hybridization – is not of great interest to the amateur gardener. But those who grow some of the gorgeous Water-lilies now available, would no doubt like to know who produced them and where they came from. Some information regarding the very popular Marliac hybrids is given on pages 64 and 65.

Few gardeners bother with the species, many of which are tender, anyway, and can't be grown out of doors.

The genus (*Nymphaea*) contains about forty species. The plants have fleshy or tuberous rootstocks. Some, such as those of the hardy kinds, are rhizomatous; others – those of the tropical kinds – are tuberous. A number of Water-lilies are viviparous, that is, they produce young plants ready to be used for new stock. Most gardeners refer to the various kinds of root stocks simply as roots.

Nymphaea are mostly natives of the Northern Hemisphere or the Tropics. A few are found in South Africa and Australia; none in New Zealand – the most beautiful perhaps come from India and are too tender for our gardens.

The colours range from white to rose, yellow and blue, and many are fragrant.

Grouped sometimes with *Nymphaea* are the gigantic *Victoria amazonica* from the lakes of tropical America (genus *Victoria*, consisting of 1 or 2 species only) and the elegant *Nelumbo*, a genus consisting of 2 hardy aquatic plants, natives of North America, Asia and Australia. These two plants are namely *Nelumbo lutea*, the American Lotus (Water Chinkapin) and *N. nucifera*, the East Indian Lotus introduced here in 1787. It is not the famous Lotus of the tropics of the Old World, which was revered by the ancient Egyptians: this plant is a *Nymphaea*, viz. *N. lotus*, introduced into Britain in 1802 and grown in special tanks in a hot-house. Plenty of information is available about this plant – in fact a whole chapter could be written on it. (See page 11.)

It is the Sacred Lily of the ancient Egyptians, whose gods are often depicted sitting on the open flower in carvings and mural paintings in tombs. Sir J. G. Wilkinson, the eminent Egyptologist ways, 'Ehôon, the Egyptian God of Day, is thus represented on the ancient monuments. He is then supposed to signify the sun in the winter solstice, or the rising sun; and the crook and flagellum (whip, scourge), the emblems of Osiris, which he sometimes carries, may be intended to indicate the influence he is about to exercise upon mankind. The vase from which the plant grows is a lake of water, and the usual initial of the word *ma* or *moo*, water.'

It was the flower worn by the Egyptians in garlands on their heads and as precious to them as were their jewelled tiaras. The flower, large, tinged with pink or red at the base, and with yellow stamens and green sepals, is much more striking than our own wild Water-lily, *Nymphaea alba*.

N. alba is a native of Europe, found in lakes or still water and slow rivers, and according to some botanists (Bentham and Hooker) it occurs in 'Central Asia, and in North Africa and North-West America.' It is mentioned in Gerarde's Herbal (1597). 'The white water Lily or Nenuphar, with great round leaves, in the shape of a buckler.' (Small round shield, usually held by hand.)

N. alba is too large and not really attractive enough for garden pools. A charming flower in nature when it is fully open in the sun at midday and surrounded by its dark green leaves. Like most of the hardy kinds, it begins to close its flowers towards the late afternoon. And if you pick them then, you will find them spattered and often soiled by water. Water-lilies must be gathered for indoor decoration early in the day. There are ways of keeping the blooms fully open; the usual method is described at the end of this chapter (page 72).

The Water-lilies included here are all suitable for small or for medium-sized pools, and a number are small enough for tubs. Some of the finest of the hybrids were raised at Temple-sur-

Lot in the South of France towards the end of the last century by M. Bory Latour Marliac, who worked assiduously for many years on the species and varieties he had collected and grew in his nurseries.

Apparently he was inspired by the researches of Professor Lévêque, the great authority on the Nymphaea, especially after reading his learned paper published in 1858 on some exotic *Nymphaea* that had been introduced into France and were growing in tanks at the Museum of Natural History in Paris. Marliac worked for a long time unsuccessfully but finally produced in 1879 the magnificent *Nymphaea* × *marliacea* Var. ROSEA (see page 56). Many other beautiful hybrids followed and were soon in much demand, for they vied with any of the gorgeous exotic greenhouse varieties and moreover were completely hardy.

AURORA, raised by Marliac in 1895, is one of the smallest hybrids, suitable for shallow water 6 to 12 inches deep. It is a lovely plant, the flowers opening yellow, then changing to orange the following day and finally to dark red. The leaves are mottled and a good foil to the flowers.

BRAKLEYI ROSEA is a charming deep pink fragrant Water-lily whose flowers are goblet-shaped and stand just above the water. The foliage is deep green and contrasts well with the rich pink. Suitable for medium-sized or large pools. I have seen it covering an area of about 8 square feet on lakes.

N. candida is a hardy species with small white flowers, smaller than in *N. alba*; it is found in Europe as far north as the Arctic countries and in Asia. It succeeds where our native species grows, but will do well in quite shallow water (6 inches deep or less) and in restricted spaces. The stigma (the top of the pistil) is scarlet and adds to the attraction of the flower.

CONQUEROR (a Marliac hybrid introduced in 1910). This variety flowers very freely and the blooms are large, a brilliant red stained with white in the interior. They look lovely at midday on the deep green leaves. It is a strong-growing Water-lily and perhaps best in a fairly big pool.

ELLISIANA (Marliac). A lovely plant carrying small vermilion-red blooms with a conspicuous bunch of orange stamens. I have seen this Water-lily growing in a nook or bay of a slow-running stream. The bay was made by digging out soil from the bank. The water should be about 12 inches deep.

Photo H. Smith

—*Photo H. Smith*

Ranunculus bullatus. A rather tender plant which grows 6-12 inches high.

9   Ranunculas Lingua. Roots densely fibrous stems 2 to 3 feet.

—*Photo H. Smith*

—*Photo H. Smith*

)   Primula Denticulata.

11   Iris Kaempferi.

12

Lysichitum americanum and Primula rosea in Savill Gardens.

N. fennica is a hardy species, a native of Finland, where it flourishes in cold, icy water. It is seldom seen in Britain, our waters not being cold enough for it, probably; but I imagine it would prosper in pools and ponds fed by a spring. The flowers are small, cut-shaped and pure white; the green leaves are also small – a charming little Water-lily for a small pool.

FIRECREST. An American hybrid with lovely pink fragrant flowers. It is one of many offered by Hillier and Sons of Winchester; and described by them as 'Free-flowering, an unusual shade of rose-pink with prominent orange stamens.' It costs about 25s. A medium-sized grower, suitable for a small pool.

FROEBELI, raised by Froebel of Zürich, is a seedling of *N. alba rubra* and has medium-sized wine-crimson flowers and large olive-green leaves; the flowers are delightfully fragrant and rise above the surface of the water. A choice Water-lily for a small pool or a tub. It costs about 15s. 6d. a root.

GONNERE (Marliac) is a very free flowering hybrid, which blooms intermittently all the summer. The large snow-white flowers are stained green and have a centre of golden-yellow stamens. It needs plenty of room and is best in a biggish pool.

GRAZIELLA (Marliac) has small reddish-copper flowers, the colour changing to orange-yellow later in the season; the leaves are attractively marked with purple. A lovely plant for small pools or tubs.

JAMES BRYDON (raised by Dreer of the U.S.A.). This is a favourite Water-lily with gardeners. It is suitable for tubs, small pools and large pools and can be grown in water 1 to 2 feet deep. The large flowers are paeony-shaped, and rich rose-crimson colour; the leaves purplish-green. It is described in many catalogues as having 'large, cup-shaped, rosy-pink flowers.'

The Laydekeri Group contains a fine choice of Water-lilies suitable for small pools or tubs. These hybrids were raised by Marliac, who, it is believed, used the species *Nymphaea tetragona* (with small white fragrant flowers) as one of the parents. (See page 68.) The name Laydekeri commemorates Marliac's son-in-law Maurice Laydeker.

LAYDEKERI FULGENS has rich red fragrant flowers with deeper red stamens. Very free flowering and continuous – ideal for a tub. Hilliers describe it as having 'flowers of medium size . . .

C

rich deep red with fiery-red stamens.' Cost: about 15s. 6d. a plant.

LAYDEKERI LILACEA. A popular variety for tub cultivation. It has medium-sized flowers, sweetly-scented, which open soft rose and white and, as they age, turn a lovely rose-crimson colour.

LAYDEKERI PURPUREA. The freest flowering of this Group of Water-lilies and in bloom longer than most of the hardy varieties, usually from June to October. The flowers, medium-sized, are a deep crimson, touched with white and star-shaped. A well-established plant will produce hundreds of blooms during a season.

MARGUERITE LAPLACE (Marliac). Like the above hybrid, this Water-lily blooms throughout the summer, and carries large, open flowers of a deep rose colour. The leaves are a reddish-brown at first, and turn green later. This variety is suitable for large and moderate-sized pools.

MARLIACEA ALBIDA (Marliac) has large white flowers – described by Hillier and Sons as 'milky-white, with prominent golden stamens; fragrant, early and free. Foliage dark green.' The flowers stand just above the water and look especially beautiful against the dark green foliage beneath. The plant costs about 15s. 6d.

MARLIACEA CARNEA. This is an exceptionally fine hybrid of Marliac's and an exceptionally strong grower, with large, open flowers of a charming shade of bluish-white stained with rose. When transplanted, the flowers are invariably pure white the first year. Suitable for medium-sized pools.

MASANIELLO (Marliac) carries large paeony-shaped flowers, sweetly scented, of a delightful shade of rich carmine-rose. Described by Hilliers as 'deep-pink splashed with carmine.' The stamens are orange-yellow. A lovely flower for a medium-sized pool.

MRS. RICHMOND (Marliac) has attractive light-green foliage and large flowers of pale rose-pink, which change to deep rose with age. The stamens are golden-yellow. The big globular flowers look best growing on their own.

N. nitida is a species from Siberia and has white, scentless, cup-shaped flowers which bloom about June. It prospers in a tub, in quite shallow water and was introduced into England about 1809.

N. odorata is the white, fragrant Water-lily of North America, where it grows in lakes and slow-moving water. The leaves are pale green. This species is better for the average garden pool than our own *N. alba*. *N. odorata* is the parent of many beautiful hybrids, several raised by Marliac.

ODORATA SULPHUREA is one of these. It is quite a small plant and suitable for a miniature pool or tub. This popular Water-lily has dark olive-green leaves heavily mottled reddish-brown – a charming setting for the numerous sulphur-yellow flowers.

ODORATA WILLIAM B. SHAW (raised by Dreer of America) has large open flowers of a rich creamy pink colour with an apricot flush. They stand well above the water. A magnificent Water-lily for planting on its own in a smallish pool, and more expensive than most – cost is about 25s. a root.

PAUL HARIOT (Marliac). This is a variety which is a favourite with many gardeners today, for it doesn't take up much room (suitable for a tub) and it flowers very freely. The blooms are of moderate size, globular, opening a soft coppery-rose and changing with age to a deep copper-red. The green leaves are spotted with maroon. It grows well in 12 inches of water or less.

N. pygmaea alba is the smallest of all the Water-lilies – a hardy species with tiny pure white scented flowers (2 inches across), which are carried very freely all through the summer. The plant may be grown in a bowl placed on a sunny window-sill. The water should be about 6 inches deep; the tubers need 4 inches of soil.

N. × pygmaea helvola is a pretty, miniature hybrid form raised by Marliac. Its tiny sulphur-yellow flowers come in profusion all the summer; and, like the preceding plant, it will grow in a bowl, say, 10 inches across, in a sunny window.

RENE GERARD (Marliac). A choice rich rose-coloured variety; the flowers are often 9 inches wide, star-shaped and the petals striped and splashed with crimson-red. Very free-flowering.

ROBINSONI (Marliac). A water-lily highly recommended by growers principally, I think, because it has a long blooming period – more hours than most during the day. The flowers are an attractive colour: yellow suffused with rose-red. The foliage is marked with maroon. Excellent for small pools and needs about a foot of water.

ROSE ARCY has star-shaped flowers, the petals slightly incurved. The colour a charming self pink. One of its great attractions is its fragrance.

ROSE NYMPH (raised by Junge and often listed in catalogues under its German name, viz., ROSEN-NYMPHE). Praised by all growers of the hardy hybrids and regarded by many gardeners as the loveliest of them. The flowers are large (7 inches across), fragrant and an enchanting shade of rose-pink. The pale green leaves harmonize beautifully with this colour.

SOLFATARE (Marliac). Yellow flowers touched with pink; the leaves beautifully marked with brownish-red. A good Water-lily for a small pool.

SUNRISE. Described by every collector and grower of hardy Water-lilies as the finest and most beautiful of all the yellow varieties. It is an American plant; the flowers are fragrant, large, soft yellow when they open and become a deeper glowing shade as the flowers expand. The green leaves are mottled brown and purple. It is suitable for medium and small pools.

N. tetragona is a species with tiny flowers, white with golden-yellow stamens; sometimes the flowers are fragrant. This little species is widely distributed in America, Asia and Australia. Introduced into Britain in 1805 but not very well known. It is not showy, of course, and it may not survive long spells of intensely cold weather. It is listed as hardy, but the roots need a good depth of water (about 12 inches, say), to escape the effects of severe frosts. The leaves are dark green mottled reddish-brown when young; dull red beneath. The flowers set seed readily enough and young plants can be raised therefore the same season.

N. tuberosa rosea is a plant many growers like for its scent (the flowers are a pale rose); it is best kept for largish pools since it is apt to spread rapidly and cover too much space.

WILLIAM FALCONER (Dreer). The darkest red Water-lily there is. The flowers are often 7 inches wide and have deep yellow stamens, which stand out conspicuously against the blood-red petals. The leaves are first a dull reddish-brown and turn green as they mature.

The few hardy species of Water-lily described here are sometimes planted in slow-running streams when these flow through a garden; they can't be compared in beauty of colour and form with any of the gorgeous hybrids and are seldom seen in the modern garden. Our own *N. alba* is perhaps the best of them (or the so-called Yellow Water-lily, *Nuphar lutea*). Those who have a riverside garden sometimes grow these two plants near the bank, that is, if the water is slow running and there are no deep rapid currents. One method which has been used success- fully is to establish a bed or a clump of Rushes or Reeds near the bank to break the flow of the water; it is better than planting certain weeds which too often spread and defile the water. The 'Bulrush' and the 'Reed Mace' are both suitable. Another Reed for this purpose is *Juncus effusus* var. SPIRALIS (with twisted stems) – best in shallow water, however, since it doesn't grow much above 18 inches.

These Reeds must be set some distance away from the spot where the Water-lily is to be planted, since they spread fairly rapidly. If they intrude too far, pull up the stems.

One could grow certain hybrid Water-lilies or even some of the half-hardy kinds near the bank of a stream. The latter are treated as annuals outside and have to be renewed every year. A good selection may be seen at Kew, in the Lily Pond, where they are planted annually.

Propagation of the hardy species is usually by seed – though not all of them seed freely. The other method – that used for all the hybrid forms – is by division of the roots or rhizomes. Division should be done in March or April. Seed of the hardy species is sown ¼ inch deep in loamy, leafy soil in shallow con- tainers and sunk in a pool during the spring.

The hardy Water-lilies do not, as a rule, lose all their leaves during the winter; but discoloured ones and those that have been damaged in some way or another should be removed when the plants have finished blooming. Remove the leaf-stems as close to the roots as possible.

There are several methods used in planting Water-lilies; but before we begin, we should remember the advice given by the specialist growers: 'Plant in May or June, when the water is warmed by the sun. Never plant in deep water to start with. Deep and cold water is often fatal to newly-planted Water-lilies.'

Planting a deep lake with them would pose many problems, then, it would seem. Usually, however, the water near the bank is fairly shallow and the Water-lilies are planted there. The biggest varieties are used: placed in receptacles containing the soil and sunk to the required depth on a hillock or mound firmly made on the base of the lake; this can be a foot high or more, depending on the depth of the water. And it can be made solid and permanent by heavy stones or bricks surrounding grass turves and heavy loam. The roots of the plants will soon find their way down into this central bed of turf and loam.

Nowadays the tubers arrive from nurseries in damp moss and oiled paper which keep them moist and ready to be planted at once. Should the tubers get dry, by delayed planting, however, they must be left in water (not too cold, by the way) for a day or two.

'Never plant in deep water' – so planting an ornamental pool some time after it has been made, means it may have to be emptied. Not a difficult job when the pool is small: one can do it with a bucket or a hand-bowl. Furthermore, an occasional cleaning out like this is a good thing. The clean water, the scrubbed sides of the stone-work make the pool a salubrious place for the plants and the fish that are to live there.

Different kinds of receptacles for the tubers are used: some gardeners favour an old wicker basket, which soon rots in the water; others prefer a wire-mesh basket, which is easy to make.* Plant the tuber in a compost of two parts strong rich loam and one part well decayed manure – so old that it will powder when rubbed in the fingers. The crown of the tuber must come just above the surface of the compost, and the tuber must be kept in its place by sticks laced across the top of the soil.

The roots of the Water-lilies soon become active in late spring and will quickly establish themselves in the soil or mud at the bottom, when clay has been used for the foundation of the pool.

In a new cement pool (the usual modern type) a barrow load of soil is put on the cement bottom and made very firm by treading or ramming it down. In the middle of some old turves place the tuber, keeping it upright and with its crown protruding from the top. First, shave off all the grass you can from the turf when you cut it. Next bind the turves together with strips of strong canvas about an inch wide. Then set the encased tuber in the bed of soil, which you press very firmly round it. I use a coating or layer of clay to reinforce the sides.

Yet another method (entailing a little more work, however) is to build a brick container or chamber about 18 inches square, its depth depending on the requirements of the Water-lily chosen. Leave a space between some of the bricks when cement-

* Plastic containers are popular nowadays.

ing them together to enable the water to circulate freely. And to prevent any soil escaping from the chamber and discolouring the water, line the bricks with perforated zinc. Now add a little water, just sufficient to soak the soil; leave this for a day or two, then add more to cover the crown of the tuber to a depth of 3 to 4 inches. As the leaves grow and develop, add more water.

A method of planting used by some gardeners of my acquaintance is to put the tuber in a small fish bass (sometimes called a rush-bag – made of coarse plaited rushes), pack good rich compost tightly round the roots, leaving the shoots at the crown peeping out at the top. (Never use leaf-mould in the compost-mixture, since it soon turns sour in the water and gives off noxious gases which suffocate the tiny leaves as they form on the stems. One grower says: 'Get some good fibrous loam and mix 4 parts of it with 1 part rotted, dried cow manure. Add 1 ounce of bone-meal to one pailful of this compose.') Thread some string through the top of the bag to keep the contents secure; it is then placed at the bottom of the pool and the water added in the usual way. For a deep pool or a lake, it must be lowered gradually into the water over a period of some weeks; as soon as the leaves are well developed and floating, let it sink to the bottom.

For a tub or half a barrel sunk in the ground in which only tiny Lilies can be grown, a good firm foundation of soil enclosed by turves or perhaps stones is all that is wanted. Plant the tuber in the soil bed, spreading out the roots to their fullest extent.

Water-lilies are hungry plants and need feeding every spring. Special fertilizers can be obtained from nurseries; these are mixed with water, made up into balls and inserted into the surrounding soil. This is an easier method than using any kind of animal manure.

Pests attack Water-lilies and other aquatics as they do any other plant. Fish help to keep the water clean and the plants in good condition. As regards the lilies, fish eat up the larvae which live on the undersides of the leaves. Goldfish are the favourites, of course, and these and other suitable forms of animal life for stocking pools and lakes are described in chapter 12, page 151. Black-fly on leaves and flower-buds should be syringed off as soon as they appear.

All dead leaves, stems, and flower-heads must be removed. Little actual pruning is necessary for most Water-lilies, however. The leaves may grow too thickly on some varieties, forcing the lilies to rise an inch or so out of the water, as, for instance, the flowers do in the hybrid COL. A. J. WELCH (see page 57). Superabundance of foliage is undesirable especially in small pools, and thinning should be done as the lily-buds begin to form. Cut off the leaf-stems as close to the roots as you can. With plenty of surface space, the flowers will then float naturally on the water. The tender species and hybrids usually carry their flowers well above the water (see page 73).

Water-lilies are magnificent flowers for indoor decoration. They look best displayed in a large, deep, cut-glass bowl, the pure crystal according well with the type of flower.

The time for picking the lilies is in the morning when they are fully open; it is likewise the best time to see them growing in the garden; they haven't much to show in the afternoon.

Some florists use different kinds of melted wax or grease on the cut blooms to keep them permanently open. It is a rather delicate operation and destructive if the wax is applied too hot – above 113°F. Paraffin-wax, sealing-wax, candle-grease, ordinary lard and other ointment-like substances which harden quickly have been used. The melted wax is dropped through a pipette-like instrument or from a small heated spoon on to the lowest parts of the sepals, petals and stamens; this sets or fixes the various organs of the flower and thus prevents the petals from moving and closing up. The smaller, richly coloured lilies are best for cutting for bowls; best of all, though, and the most beautiful, are the tender kinds we grow in the greenhouse.

Good roots of Water-lilies can be obtained from any nursery specializing in aquatics, such as Hillier and Sons, Winchester, and Highlands Water Gardens, Rickmansworth, Hertfordshire.

CHAPTER FIVE

Some Tender Water-lilies

Many tender exotic flowers are grown out of doors in our gardens. But they live only a few months as annuals and die off with the fall of the year when left in the open. Most of our border annuals succumb to the cold and new plants are put out again the following season. Occasionally, more venturesome gardeners sink in their borders pots of things like showy Cinerarias; Schizanthus (Butterfly Flowers); Gloxinias (all in full bloom and straight from the greenhouse): and they carefully cover the rims of the pots with soil to give the plants the appearance of growing directly in the border.

We can also grow some of the gorgeous tropical Water-lilies in the garden, bringing them from the greenhouse and planting them in our pools. And we plant them out about the same time as we do the tender, pot-grown flowers: when there is no risk of frosts and, of course, when the water has lost its winter chill.

Tender Water-lilies are grown outside in the Lily Pond at Kew Botanic Gardens,* and are treated as annuals, new roots or tubers being raised every year.

Those who have seen them growing there will have noticed that they carry their flowers well above the water. The flowers of the *hardy* varieties float, though a superabundance of leaves may cause the flowers to stand out of the water, as those of our native *N. alba* do, and also those of the hardy variety COL. A. J. WELCH (see page 57). Normally, however, the position of the flowers is a method of determining the relative hardiness of the various species and hybrids.

In pools in a heated greenhouse, there is no difficulty in flowering the tropical *Nymphaea* successfully. The right temperature is there, and the closed place and warm atmosphere bring out the wonderful scents, and also enable us to enjoy the beauty of the nocturnal kinds which begin to open just after dusk. We

* This pond was made from an old gravel pit in 1897.

can, of course, enjoy them outside in mid-summer, but the weather may be bad, and the fragrance of the flowers is not so readily perceived in the open air.

It is possible to have a pool outside with heated water. Different methods are used to keep the water at the correct temperature. McIntosh, the landscape gardener, writing in 1838, talks vaguely of a 'water-basin garden,' which could grow half-hardy plants 'if the water supply was connected to the hot water system of the house.' Presumably this would be done with pipes leading into the pool and fixed round the inside. But few people could afford to have a pool with such an elaborate heating system installed.

At Waddesdon Manor, when the late Mr. James de Rothschild lived there, a beautiful blue tropical Water-lily was grown in a partly enclosed tank attached to one of the hot-houses, the heated water being easily supplied by pipes running from the main greenhouse. The lilies were principally grown for cutting for indoor decoration.

Given the right temperature and the room, indoor cultivation of tropical *Nymphaeas* is a simple matter. The tubers are started in March in a compost of 2 parts rich turfy loam and 1 part well-decayed manure; they are put erect in pots (one tuber to a pot), the compost packed round them and then immersed under 6 inches of water in tubs or containers exposed to full sunlight. The temperature of the greenhouse as from March to September should be 65° to 75°F.; that of the water about 65°F. As soon as the leaves develop and are floating, the tubs can be lowered into the tanks or pool in the floor where they are to grow and flower through the season. More water is added till the right depth is obtained.

One of the smaller varieties such as the hybrid DAUBENYANA, which has light blue flowers and blooms very freely all through the summer and autumn, is ideally suited to specimen cultivation in a tub – or half a barrel – in the cool greenhouse, or sunk in the ground outdoors when the weather is warm enough. Or it can of course be grown in a heated pool. Knock the tuber out of the pot when new growth commences and plant it at the bottom of the tub in 12 inches of compost, under which is a thin layer of well-rotted manure. Plant firmly and add sufficient warm water just to cover the crown. DAUBENYANA does best in shallow water – 3 or 4 inches deep. And according to one specialist, it will flower continuously for seven years in a heated greenhouse. A choice blue-flowered plant for the winter months! It is one of the viviparous forms and produces on its small floating leaves bulbils, from which new plants are grown (see page 80).

It will be necessary to keep the temperature at about 60°F. through the winter if flowers are wanted during that period. More often than not the heat is lowered and the tubers are removed from the water when the foliage begins to die back; they are stored in damp sand in a temperature of 50°F. or more till the following March, when they are planted again.

I've found that the easiest way of growing tropical Water-lilies in a greenhouse is to plant them in containers filled with compost and sink them gradually into the tank or the pool and leave them there till the autumn, when the heat is turned down; they are there removed without any difficulty (without having to drain the tank); and the soil can be changed when the tubers are replanted the following spring. They are dried and stored in the usual way.

This method can be used for planting them in the garden-pool. When the weather is warm enough, the containers are gradually sunk into the pool; if the place is sunny and sheltered the plants will soon begin to grow. It is necessary to stand the containers on a mound of bricks or on a tall, upturned flower-pot so that they are not plunged immediately into deep water.

The first cold spell will cause the leaves to wither; the plants are then removed from the pool and the tubers discarded.

The tender species are mostly natives of Tropical America, Egypt, India, the East Indies and of Australasia. Many of the loveliest hybrids were raised in the U.S.A., where they are more widely grown than in Britain. (One of the chief raisers there was Mr. George Pring of the Missouri Botanic Garden.) Although many bloom at night, they often remain open till midday.

Tropical Water-lilies are not widely grown by amateur gardeners, for they don't like the trouble of planting fresh tubers every year. But those who have a greenhouse, might like to try one or two, using perhaps a tub or half a barrel as a container.

Some of the best and most desirable are described in the following pages. Others will be found in the supplementary list of aquatics, pages 162–163. The nocturnal or night-blooming hybrids are given separately, since people who have hot-houses and grow any of the tropical kinds at all usually find these the most interesting.

Nymphaea amazonum comes from Tropical America. It has heart-shaped leaves (4 to 12 inches long), reddish-brown beneath, and very fragrant yellowish-white flowers with thick, leathery petals. The flowers are quite small – about 3 inches across and bloom at night.

N. ampla, from the same part of the world, is not in cultivation. But the form Var. *speciosa* apparently is, and has white or yellowish-white flowers which bloom in July. It needs a hot-house and was introduced as long ago as 1801.

BAGDAD is a lovely tropical hybrid for a large tank. The flowers are an exquisite shade of Wisteria-blue and have deep golden stamens. The leaves are dark green spotted with brown.

N. burtii from Tanganyika (1929) is difficult to grow, but hybrids from it bloom freely and flourish in quite cool water. (ST. LOUIS is one of these, see page 78). The flowers of the species are a deep primrose, 8 inches across and fragrant.

BLUE BEAUTY (Synonym: PENNSYLVANIA). This is a fine tender lily for a small tank or a tub. It has large, open deep blue flowers with conspicuous yellow stamens. The leaves are dark green, mottled brown.

N. caerulea. Native of Northern and Central Africa. Introduced into Britain in 1812. An old Water-lily and one of the loveliest of the blue kinds. The flowers are a light blue, faintly scented and measure about 6 inches across. It thrives in a cool greenhouse. I have known gardeners plant the tubers in a container and sink it outside in a pool about mid-May, then lift it and bring it back indoors for the winter, removing the tuber or tubers and storing them in moist sand in a temperature of 55°F. But this species is best and easiest grown inside. The flowers stand well out of the water and look very beautiful above the ovalish green leaves (they are about 12 inches wide). This Nymphaea is often called the Blue Lotus of the Nile.

M. capensis is known as the Cape Blue Water-lily and is found in lakes in South and East Africa and in Madagascar. It has roundish leaves about 12 inches across and beautiful bright blue, fragrant flowers. It blooms freely and is easy to grow in a heated greenhouse. The variety *zanzibariensis* (from Zanzibar) is a darker shade of blue, and its anthers are shaded violet; the flowers are delightfully fragrant.

CASTALLIFLORA was raised by George Pring in 1913 by crossing two pink forms of *N. c. zanzibariensis Var. rosea*. The flowers are pale pink, often 10 inches wide, and have yellow stamens. The leaves are mottled with red.

DAUBENYANA (raised by Dauben) is a favourite tender hybrid for planting in a garden pool round about the end of May (see page 74). The flowers are blue and quite small. A useful viviparous form.

DEVONIENSIS was raised in 1851 at Chatsworth, the country seat of the Duke of Devonshire, and named in honour of him. One of the parents was the deep red *N. rubra* from Bengal. The hybrid plant has larger flowers (often 12 inches in diameter) and of a brilliant rose-red colour. They stand well out of the water, above the bronze-red leaves.

DIRECTOR GEORGE T. MOORE. A very free-flowering hybrid with rich deep purple, medium-sized flowers; the green leaves are an excellent foil.

EMILY GRANT HUTCHINGS (an American hybrid). A deep amaranth-pink lily, cup-shaped and large – sometimes described as bell-shaped. I have seen it blooming at night. (Amaranth, by the way, is a purplish colour.)

N. gigantea is a native of Australia and one of the most beautiful of all the blue Water-lilies. Sky-blue flowers, 6 or 7 inches across, with golden stamens. Much larger flowers than this, however, have been recorded. It is one of the species that is grown outside in heated pools. Introduced in 1852.

HENRY SHAW (raised by George Pring). A favourite tropical hybrid; a strong, vigorous grower needing plenty of room. It has large, bright blue flowers which come abundantly all the summer.

N. lotus (see page 63). The leaves are large, peltate (shield-shaped, with the stems attached to the centre); the flowers, 5 to 10 inches across, scentless, white or tinged with pink or red at the base of the petals. The stamens are golden-yellow. The seeds and tubers are edible and used as food in parts of Africa. The ancient Egyptians used to dry them and grind them down into flour to make a sort of coarse bread.

N. pubescens is a tender species, a native of India, Java and the Philippines, and one of those recommended for growing in an aquarium to provide shade for tropical fish. The leaves are dark green above and purplish beneath, the flowers small and white with greenish sepals. In India the tubers and seeds are also used for food.

MRS. C. W. WARD carries its large, rich rose-pink flowers well above the water. The golden-yellow stamens stand out conspicuously against the rich pink.

MRS. EDWARD WHITTAKER (Pring). This has large lavender-blue flowers, with deep yellow stamens. It must be given protection and grows well in a tub.

MRS. GEORGE PRING (raised by Pring in 1922). A beautiful pure white tropical hybrid with pointed petals and bronze-golden stamens tipped with purple. Delightfully fragrant.

PANAMA PACIFIC. This is among the easiest of the tender varieties to grow. The flowers are a singularly beautiful shade of rose-purple, suffused with amaranth. They stand well above the water. A viviparous form.

N. rubra is a lovely night-blooming species from India, with deep red flowers, 5 to 8 inches across. The leaves, purplish-red at first, become greener as they mature. It is one of the parents of the ever lovelier hybrid DEVONIENSIS (see page 77).

N. stellata. A native of South and East Asia and has pale blue star-shaped flowers, 3 to 7 inches across. There are pink and white forms and the most decorative is the sky-blue Var. BERLIN, which will bloom outside all the summer if grown in a specially heated pool.

ST. LOUIS (raised by Pring in 1930). A hybrid from *N. burtii*. A rare yellow lily. A soft yellow shade and very attractive. The stamens are a deep golden-yellow and add to the beauty of the flower, which is large and star-shaped. The green leaves are mottled with bronze.

There are many night-blooming *Nymphaea*; all of them lovely, and the beauty of their colouring is enhanced by artificial light, though this should never be glaring – some form of indirect lighting is best. The red varieties are the most striking.

ARMAND MILLET is a brilliant red-purple; the flowers are large and stand out well against the deep green toothed leaves.

FRANK TRELEASE was raised by Gurney in 1900 and is one of the most popular of the night-blooming hybrids. The dark crimson colour is its great attraction. The stamens are a darker shade of red and the large, olive-green leaves are a perfect foil.

GEORGE HUSTER (raised in America). A magnificent Water-lily at night. The rich red velvety flowers become a lustrous crimson.

JUNO has many large creamy-white flowers with broad petals; the stamens form a conspicuous golden-yellow centre.

LA REINE DE LOS ANGELES (raised in 1935) is one of the white varieties and a very beautiful flower for displaying in the dusk without any light, for the flowers show up magnificently, giving an enchanting black-and-white effect.

MINERVA. Another white. Pure white, large flowers which are singularly lovely in the twilight.

MISSOURI (raised by Pring in 1933). Yet another white variety. The flowers are very large (some over 12 inches across) and stand up out of the water, on their long thick stems. Very beautiful in a subdued light.

PRIDE OF CALIFORNIA (raised in 1935) is a favourite night-blooming hybrid in the United States and often grown outside in the warmest gardens along the Pacific coast. The colour is a deep red and startlingly beautiful when seen by floodlighting – a popular way of illuminating gardens in many parts of America, especially those in the warm southern districts on the Pacific seaboard. (Even more fascinating is underwater lighting! Special lamps for submerging in the pool cost about £10 and are easily installed. Blue, green, yellow and pink colours are available. Choice of colour should depend on the colour of the flowers grown in the pool: for instance, green wouldn't be good with red ones. Both green and blue are cold colours. Pink or red is warm – particularly beautiful with white flowers. And the safest flowers to be illuminated with this lighting are of course white ones.)

RUFUS J. LACKLAND, our last variety, has large deep crimson flowers which become more purplish toward the end of the season. Like many of these hybrids, it needs feeding during the growing season. In a pool, in which only the lilies grow, there is no difficulty: feed the plants occasionally with a little liquid manure. But where there are different kinds of fish and other creatures living, it would be wise to use manures or fertilizers prescribed by aquatic specialists. Firms selling aquaria, fish, oxygenating plants and mollusca will supply full information on this matter.

These night-blooming hybrids are vigorous plants and need plenty of room in which to develop. The smallest pool should not be under 12 feet in diameter.

The sweetly-scented *N. amazonum* and one or two other small-ish species are sometimes grown in tubs and will thrive and flower well if fed regularly with weak doses of liquid manure.

It is easy to propagate the tropical species from seed. (This is best harvested before the pods burst, otherwise it will be scattered on the water and after a short time sink to the bottom of the pool and be lost.)

Sow the seeds about ⅛ inch deep in a shallow pan of rich loan and crushed charcoal; barely cover them with water and keep in a temperature of about 70°F. till they germinate. The seedlings are potted up, then placed in shallow water and, as they develop, submerged into deeper water. Many will flower the same season.

Tropical Water-lilies that bear viviparous leaves may be propagated by detaching these from the plants and pegging them down into shallow pans of soil with a little water. The old leaf will eventually rot and leave the new plant well rooted in the soil.

13
Primula pulverulenta "Bartley Strain".

14 Alopecurus pratensis var. Aureus,
an attractive foliage-plant.

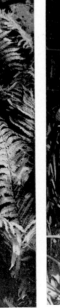

15
Matteuccia Struthiopteris. Needs damp
conditions for its roots all the year round.

16
Narcissus Bulbocodium.

Photo H. Smith

17

Formal pool with fountain. Not suitable for Water-Lilies.

18
Cypripedium reginae. A hardy orchid for the Bog-garden.
—Photo H. Smith

—Photo H. Smith

19
Trollius, Springhill Beauty.

20　An unusually long shaped pond.

—*Photo L. E. Perkins*

21　Lily Amabilis.

CHAPTER SIX

The Giant Water-lily and
Some Other Kinds

ONE Water-lily very few of us can grow is *Victoria amazonica* or *Victoria regia* as it is better known. This is an enormous aquatic with leaves often 6 feet across. Like the Redwood of California, it is one of the gargantuan plants of the vegetable kingdom. It is essentially an exhibition-plant for the collector and the Botanic Gardens.

It needs a tank at least 6 feet deep and 25 or 30 feet wide filled, according to one grower, with running water which must be maintained at a temperature of 80°F. and the hot-house should never be under 75°F. which knocks most of us out, I imagine. Nonetheless, many garden-instruction books give detailed information on how to grow it. It needs 'a compost of 2 parts good turfy loam, 1 part decayed cow manure. . . . Plant in May. . . . No shade required. Propagate by seeds in a pot of sandy loam submerged in water heated to a temperature of 85°F. . . . The *Victoria regia* is strictly a perennial, but thrives best treated as an annual in this country.' (T. W. Sanders. *Encyclopedia of Gardening.*)

Very fine specimens can be seen in the hot-houses at many Botanic Gardens. No doubt most garden-lovers in the London district will have visited Kew to see the lily there in bloom in House No. 10 of the T Range of Glasshouses (the temperature is about 70°F.) It blooms in late summer, and the best time to see the flowers is late afternoon or evening. A gardener tells me that the seed is sown in January in pots and the pot containing the seedling, when big enough, is put into the tank at the beginning of June. Three months later the surface is covered with leaves 6 feet across.

Equally fine specimens can be seen in private collections in this country. And the first was flowered at Chatsworth in 1849 by Joseph Paxton, the famous gardener and horticulturist (later Sir Joseph Paxton).

This giant Water-lily was discovered in Bolivia in 1801, but not introduced into Britain till 1838. Sir Robert Schomburgk found it growing in a river in British Guiana, where he had been sent on an expedition for the Royal Geographical Society. It was on January 1st, 1837, and he had reached a part of the river Berbice where it widened and formed a lake-like expanse of still water. He was travelling with natives of the district in canoes and saw the lilies floating in the distance. He described his discovery as 'a vegetable wonder.' The gigantic leaves were 5 to 6 feet across, flat, with a broad rim, 3 or 4 inches deep – the colour was light green above and vivid crimson beneath. They floated on the water, which was smooth and covered with flowers which measured 12 inches in diameter. The flower, when it first unfolds, is white, with a pink centre. 'The colours spread," Schomburgk wrote, 'as the bloom increases in age, and at a day old, the whole is rose-coloured. As if to add to the charm of this noble Water-lily, it diffuses a sweet scent.'

Seeds were sent in bottles of fresh water to England and eventually plants were raised and flowered in 1849. The plant created a sensation at Chatsworth and the event was celebrated by an elaborate entertainment there. An exciting moment occurred when little Miss Paxton, dressed as a fairy was carefully deposited on a flat board on one of the wide, tea-tray leaves!

The lily was named in honour of Queen Victoria. The correct specific name is *Victoria amazonica*, the name first given to it; but it is more often called *Victoria regia*.

There is another species, viz. *V. trickeri*, which appears to be hardier than *V. amazonica* and will thrive in a greenhouse with a temperature of 55°F. It resembles the other plant, but has lighter green leaves with purple undersides. Introduced into cultivation towards the end of the nineteenth century.

At Kew Botanic Gardens there is also in the *Victoria amazonica* tank another Water-lily, namely *Eurayle ferox*, which has large flat leaves but without an upturned rim. The leaves are circular, about 2 feet across, spiny, olive-green above and rich purple beneath; the flowers are a deep violet colour and bloom in September; they are, however, surprisingly small, not more than 2 inches across.

The plant produces berries 2 to 4 inches across, which in India are roasted and eaten. (Another interesting aquatic in this tank, by the way, is the Tropical Duck Weed, *Pistia stratiotes*, a floating plant which sends down long, feathery roots and spreads rapidly. It often covers the whole surface of a heated pool and keeps the water below fresh and cool.)

The so-called East India Lotus is a tropical Water-lily with normal-sized leaves and is sometimes grown out of doors in warm, sheltered gardens. Its specific name is *Nelumbo nucifera* (*Nelumbo* is the Cingalese name of the plant); the species is sometimes described under *Nelumbium speciosum* and listed in catalogues under *Nelumbium* (a synonym).

It has often been called the Egyptian Lotus and believed to be the Water-lily cultivated by the ancient Egyptians; but this plant is *Nymphaea lotus* described on page 77. The *Nelumbo* is the Chinese Water-lily, the sacred Flower of India and China, the flower in which Buddha and other deities sit. It has several popular names, viz. the East Indian Lotus; the Hindu Lotus and the Sacred Bean of India. But the plant, widely distributed in Asia, is no longer found in the Nile.

In ancient times *Nelumbo nucifera* seems to have been valued more as an economic plant than as an ornamental and it was very probably introduced by the Egyptians into their country from India and widely cultivated there for its many uses.

The botanist Willian Rhind, writing about it in the nineteenth century, says it is a native of China, Japan, Persia, Asiatic Russia and of both the East and West Indies. The long stalks, 2 to 6 feet high, are used in various tropical countries as food. The roots or tubers were sliced finely and used with the seeds and the kernels of apricots and walnuts in a special iced concoction served in China. And to preserve the roots for later use, they were salted down and covered with vinegar. 'The seeds,' says Rhind, 'are somewhat of the size and form of an acorn and of a taste more delicate than that of almonds.'

The leaves are an attractive glaucous colour, often wavy at the margins, and measure 2 feet or more in width. They are peltate (the stems or leafstalks inserted in the centre of the leaf, as in Nasturtium) and rise several feet out of the water. The flowers are white, tipped with rose or pink and very fragrant. They overtop the leaves and often measure 12 inches across. A most striking-looking aquatic when in full bloom. Apparently it is found copiously in the muddy marshes of China and India. In the gardens and houses of the mandarins it was cultivated in special pots and jars.

There are many variants of this plant (all very desirable); *alba* (the Magnolia Lotus) with white flowers; *alba grandiflora* with large white flowers; *alba striata* has white flowers striped and tipped with rose-pink; *pygmaea alba* is a dwarf form with leaves 6 inches wide and small white flowers; one of the most beautiful is *pekinensis rubra* with amaranth-red flowers.

Although *N. nucifera* comes through the severe winters of central China unharmed, it doesn't survive our frosts and if grown outside in a warm sheltered garden, must be brought back into the greenhouse by early October.

Nelumbo need a rich turfy soil (a mixture of 2 parts loam and 1 part well-rotted cow manure is recommended). The tubers must be planted 3 to 5 inches deep in about 10 inches of this compost. Be careful not to damage the eyes or growing points when setting the tubers in position.

Like the tropical *Nymphaea*, they may be started in pots in a heated greenhouse, then transferred to tubs and planted outside in a warm, sheltered pool in June. Depth of water should not be less than 12 inches.

Nuphar is a genus of about seven species of aquatics resembling small Water-lilies and, like the hardy varieties we grow, will thrive in ponds and pools and in slow-running streams. They are natives of the temperate regions of the northern hemisphere; and the attractive *Nuphar lutea* is found in some of our rivers, often in deep water. Its flowers are yellow, like large Buttercups, and raised slightly in the water. The leaves are lobed at the base and comparatively large – some 12 inches across. The plant is familiarly known as Brandy Bottle; the name was given to it, it is said, because the flowers have a strong alcoholic smell. It is the best known of the species (not many nurseries have others for sale) and will prosper and bloom freely in quite shallow water and actually seems to prefer it.

There are several varieties – not very well known, apparently. One of the most beautiful is Var. SERICEUM, a form with larger deeper yellow flowers; it is found in rivers and lakes in Hungary and is suitable for large, shallow pools.

Less-known species and varieties are *N. advena* from North America, a charming Water-lily-like plant with yellow flowers 2 or 3 inches wide, globular, and raised out of the water. The red anthers are striking. The leaves, erect, large, heart-shaped, stand up well above the flowers. The species is in bloom all the summer.

N. japonica, from Japan. It has large, arrow-shaped floating leaves and 3-inch wide golden-yellow flowers which are raised out of the water.

The variety RUBROTINCTUM is regarded as the finest of the *Nuphar*; it has dark olive-green leaves which stand erect out of the water and very attractive cup-shaped, orange-scarlet flowers.

N. microphylla. A miniature species from North America, with delightful submerged lettuce-like leaves. A charming plant for an aquarium where these leaves can be seen in the water. The leaves that float on the surface and the pale yellow flowers are both very small. It is sometimes planted along with the Water-lily *Nymphaea pubescens* in a glass tank stocked with tropical fish. (The *Nymphaea* is commonly known as the 'Arrowhead Water-lily,' the submerged leaves being arrow-shaped.)

Nuphar are planted in the same way as *Nymphaea*; the roots can be set in a wicker or plastic container and sunk in shallow water. A good turfy loam is an ideal planting medium.

Our cold winters do not harm any of the hardy Water-lilies we grow outside. They are unaffected by frost and snow; the ice on the ponds does not kill them, provided the roots are covered with at least 10 inches of water.

When the spring comes, remove all the rubbish and dead leaves that may have accumulated through the autumn and winter months. And if you intend draining your pool, this is the time to do it. It is the only time, too, when you can renew the soil round the rootstocks. Scrape away some of this and replace with good turfy loam.

Water-lilies are subject to certain diseases and are sometimes attacked by pests such as Black Fly and Mosquito Larvae.

One of the worst is a leaf-spot caused by a fungus. Treatment: remove all leaves and parts of leaves showing spots.

Equally destructive is a parasitic fungus which attacks the stems of Water-lilies and similar aquatics, causing a blackening and rotting away of the stems. Treatment: a weak solution of copper must be added to the water; but badly affected plants should be removed at once and destroyed by burning.

For the copper solution use 2½ ounces of copper sulphate for each 10,000 gallons of water. Put the copper into a linen bag and pull it round and round the pool till the crystals have dissolved. (To calculate the cubic content of your pool: multiply together the length, breadth and depth in feet; then multiply the result by 6 to get the approximate number of gallons.)

For Water-lily aphis, Black Fly and the like, use a contact wash of nicotine-soap or pyrethrum-extract (full instructions are supplied with these substances). Avoid any wash containing derris, since this will poison the fish. Often heavy rains will wash the insects off the leaves. And surface eating fish will quickly clear them.

Similarly, fish will feed on the eggs and larvae of the Water-lily Beetle. To make sure that they reach them, carefully hoop bent wires round the stems of the leaves to keep them submerged for a few days.

CHAPTER SEVEN

Pools for the Garden

MANY types of pools are available for the garden nowadays. It is quite possible that the old-fashioned cement-pool has gone for good, though some gardeners still like to make them; and books and articles on Water-gardens still give full instructions on how to do it.

But whatever type of pool you decide to have, you must first 'dig a hole'. 'Just dig a hole' says the heading to one advertisement. Nowadays that is perhaps the most difficult part of the job. Just did a hole and drop in a 'one-piece' hand-moulded pool; and, according to a firm who supplies all sorts of pools, 'You can be swimming in your own garden in much less time than it took to dig the hole!' And you can choose from at least half a dozen models all in everlasting fibre-glass, some of which, by the way, are designed to stand on the surface, rather like huge baths.

The ornamental pool for Water-lilies can also be made of fibre-glass and of other materials: in a few years' time there will probably be dozens of different sorts of materials to choose from. You can now have fibre-glass shells (pre-fabricated in various shapes); or plastic or butyl rubber liner (fibre-glass and this marvellous rubber composition last a lifetime); 'Gunite' – cement and sand sprayed under pressure; PVC (polyvinyl-chloride); and real stone – if you have any qualms about modern scientific materials. But if you go and see some of these ready-made pools covered with Water-lilies and stocked with goldfish you'll probably decide to have one on the spot.

Before you start any preparations, however, you must have a suitable site for a pool – ornamental or swimming; a pool in a completely shady garden is useless. The best of the flowering aquatics won't grow in shade; and nobody wants to swim where there's no sun. So you may have to fell some trees, or, if you live on the top of an exposed hill, you will be wise to enclose your garden either with a high fence or a wall to keep out the cold and protect yourself from north-east winds.

Another point to consider: you must be reasonably near your water-supply; for every so often it will be necessary to replenish the water in the pool (you may have a garden-tap, which is always useful, or you may have to use the water from the kitchen). Even during one of our ordinary summers quite a lot of water is lost by evaporation.

PUDDLED POOLS

The cement or stone pool was till recently the favourite type of ornamental pool and the oldest, excepting the puddled pool or pond (made of clay) which was the only kind known in gardens centuries ago.

Many people believe that these clay-ponds are the easiest to make: actually they are the most difficult and really a job for the expert craftsman; moreover they are more of a success in some districts than in others. There should be a natural supply of good rich clay available and the site should be on low-lying ground and the rainfall in the district high.

Making one of these pools entails more work than the usual cement pool does. The clay (usually mixed with sand) is worked with water to a thick plasticine consistency and kept moist enough to mould round the hole which has been dug. The bottom must be well rammed down to make it very firm; the sides, sloping gradually up, are similarly firmed and hardened and the whole of the basin or depression is then covered with a thick layer of straw. Failing straw, dried heather or dead rushes may be used. These materials prevent any heat from reaching the clay and causing it to crack. The puddled clay is worked into the straw and on to it till a thick smooth surface is obtained. If the pond is filled with water and kept full it will remain leak-proof for years.

This is how farmers in the past made their Dew ponds or Cloud ponds. They were made on hills and downs where there was no adequate water-supply from springs or surface-drainage, and they were fed by the condensation of water from the atmosphere.

Plants which send out long foraging roots should not be grown near a puddled pool, since the roots will eventually penetrate the clay and allow the water to escape. The safest kinds are the floating plants such as *Azolla caroliniana* from the Deep South of America. It has tiny, fleshy, fern-like leaves, bright green in the spring and reddish-bronze in the autumn. It is simply planted *on* the water and it soon spreads over the surface.

CONCRETE POOLS

If the old-fashioned puddled pool is really an expert's job, the cement-made pool is everybody's and anybody's. Making a small ornamental pool for the garden is interesting work and not too arduous even for a child.

It is an excellent week-end recreation for the sedentary man. He can take as long over it as he wishes; he can begin in the spring, spread the work out over the summer and start the cementing before the frosts begin in October. It is a job for every garden enthusiast. Winston Churchill made his own pool at Chartwell in the years preceding the war. He says in Vol. 1, *The Second World War*,* 'I built with my own hands a large part of two cottages and extensive kitchen-garden walls, and made all kinds of rockeries and water-works and a large swimming-pool which was filtered to limpidity and could be heated to supplement our feeble sunshine.' (Swimming-pool construction is discussed on page 96.)

Some gardeners first like to draw a plan of the pool they are going to make. It may be necessary where a good-sized pool – and especially a swimming-pool – is wanted. The lie of the land may present several constructional problems; and methods of providing various depths will have to be decided upon.

Normally, however, you mark out the shape on the ground roughly with some short of sharp-pointed tool and work to that pattern. Informal pools, ovalish-shaped or of an irregular design – some have a waved edge – are less difficult to prepare and line with cement than the rectangular or box-shaped kind.

INFORMAL POOLS

For an ordinary ovalish pool, measuring, say, 5 feet long, take out the soil to a depth of about 2 feet. And if you are working on your own, don't expect to accomplish the task in a single morn-

* *The Gathering Storm*, page 62.

ing: work comfortably and make arrangements beforehand where you are going to put the excavated soil: it could be spread evenly round the hole, and raked over and planted with grass seed. I can't think of anything easier or more suitable. (I certainly don't advocate piling it up somewhere to use for a rockery: rockeries, or the rocks and boulders that compose it, should always be slightly *below* the surface of the ground, not *above* it.) On the other hand, you may have to wheel the soil away to another part of the garden; this is heavy work. When the lake at Kew Gardens was excavated, the soil removed was utilized for pathways.

The bottom of the hole is covered with a layer of smallish stones which must be well rammed down to form a good solid base to take the cement and form the floor. Make sure that the base is well and truly firm, or there is a risk that the soil will sink and subsequently cause cracks in the bottom of the pool.

The concrete required is best made up of 1 part cement, 2 parts sand, and 5 parts rubble or shingle (small pieces of broken stone will do.) And you should of course do all your mixing on a board, which is much easier to work on than the ground.

Turn the dry materials over and over with a shovel to mix them thoroughly, then sprinkle the heap with water from a can with the rose attached. When you've got the mixture reasonably wet, put a 6-inch layer on the floor and work it well down with the shovel before you make it firm with a piece of flat board. A large trowel or plasterer's flat smoothing-tool will give a final good even surface. Leave it for a few hours, then sprinkle a little water over it from a watering-can – see that the rose is firm, and that you don't use too much water. Leave for several days, watering it occasionally during hot weather; it will then be hard enough to stand on.

The sloping sides need a thinner, smoother sort of concrete: use 1 part cement to 3 parts sand; do not include any stones or rubble. Before you start lining, beat the sides with the back of a spade, which will cause any loose soil to fall. Next, with a metal-pointed dibber, make holes in the sides to take some of the cement, otherwise it will not adhere and will begin to slide away from the soil. The cavities made with the dibber must be well firmed; a small stone in each will provide a 'key' for the cement, holding it firmly in position.

Use 2 layers of cement for the lining. The first, 3 inches thick, is put on with a trowel, scored with the point and left to dry for two days.

Many gardeners at this stage like to add some sort of reinforcement, say, large mesh galvanized chicken-wire; it is certainly necessary when building a large pool.

The mesh-wire is placed on the base over a 3-inch layer of wet concrete and spread out and up the sides, on the scored layer, so that the whole basin is practically lined with the wire. Pieces can be cut out and secured to the large piece to cover every square inch. Then the second 3-inch layer of concrete is spread over the wire to cover it and come up the sides to a height of about 6 inches. This method gives a good strong joint at the point where the floor and the sides meet. The lining (with the thinner cement) is then continued in the normal way, the second 3-inch layer being spread over the wire and smoothed with the blade of the trowel and left to set hard. After 24 hours it may be filled with water. (Fig. 4 shows section of informal cement pool.)

But most builders prefer to paint over this second surface a cement grout (equal parts of cement and fine sand mixed with water to a thick cream), which usually prevents cracks forming.

And a method of insulating the water from the concrete, which in its fresh limy state is inimical to plants and pond-life, is to paint on two coats of a solution made of 1 part of waterglass to 4 parts of water.

Special preparations such as plastics for filling cracks, semi-plastic sealing coats, and semi-liquid priming coats can be bought at any Water-garden nurseries. The substance called 'Gandersil' is excellent for sealing and waterproofing new concrete. It is simply dissolved in water and brushed on to the surface. Let it dry for 24 hours. Then rinse out the pool, mop it dry and fill up with fresh water. The pool is then ready for planting and stocking with fish.

Another method is to fill the pool in the autumn – in September, if you can – and leave it till spring. It is then emptied and refilled, and in the spring is perfectly safe for planting.

'What is the best medium for planting?' A coarse heavy loam is ideal. It should be about 6 inches deep and placed on a layer of well-rotted cow manure (at least a year old). Other kinds, such as pig, poultry, etc., are not suitable. Ram the loam down well and sprinkle with small stones or pebbles. Leave to settle for a day or two. You can then plant your aquatics, adding a little water at a time until the pool is filled.*

The water must be added gradually. In a small pool this is simple; just use a watering-can. For a big pool use a hosepipe and fill up slowly; let the water from a fine sprayer reach the surface at an angle.

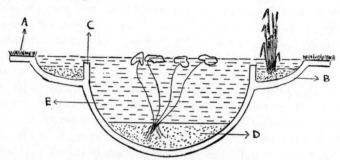

Fig. 4. Shows section of informal pool

A = grass verge   D = soil
B = concrete lining   E = water
C = miniature concrete wall to support soil on ledge

Small pools, such as most of us will build, scarcely need an outlet pipe at the base for draining away the water when we want to change it; neither is an overflow pipe necessary. The usual method of changing the water and/or refreshing it, is to hose it very gently with the pipe attached to the kitchen tap. A fine 'mist' sprayer or rose fixed to the pipe, which is placed at an angle of about 45° at the side of the pool, will provide a gentle flow of water into the pool, and will not disturb the plants or the fish. After about 10 minutes turn off the water and let the pool rest. Recommence later and continue in this way till the water is renewed. Never change the water quickly or the temperature will drop and harm or perhaps kill whatever is living in the pool.

In a natural setting of grass the overflow is soon absorbed and drains away into the ground. The quantity in a small pool isn't large, anyway, and can scarcely make the grass soggy. Actually it will improve it.

A surround of paving stones for an informal pool, especially one unusually irregular in shape, looks out of place and is not

* Large pools often take weeks to fill, a little water being added each week.

recommended. Grass growing right up to the edge, or *down* to it, is best – the cement top should come 2 inches below the surface of the ground.

Paving stones, however, may be set in the grass here and there near the edge and used as stepping-stones to prevent the grass being worn bare.

FORMAL POOLS

The construction of a formal or a rectangular pool entails much more labour upon the builder. For even the smallest, with its vertical sides (say, 18 inches deep), needs a wooden framework fitted round the sides to support the wet concrete walls. It is a sort of mould and must be strong enough to stand the pressure of the concrete, especially the amount required to line a big pool.

But first the floor is made and laid in the same way as that for an informal pool; for a wide floor (6 feet or more) you will need a large, heavy piece of wood for tamping (ramming down); and it is important to get the surface perfectly even, otherwise in the course of time the soil base will move naturally to any lower part or hollow. Check every so often with a spirit-level.

The wooden box-like framework erected in the excavated hole (6 inches from the sides) consists simply of horizontal boards kept firmly in position by strong upright posts, to which they are nailed. The posts (inside the framework) are supported by wooden braces running across from one to the other. (See Fig. 5.)

Most builders grease the outsides of the boards to prevent the wet concrete adhering, and to facilitate the removal of the wooden structure when the concrete has set.

You can use one of the proprietary brands of mould-oil, or a mixture made up of 75 per cent paraffin oil and 25 per cent raw linseed oil.

Many gardeners like to have a ledge or shelf round the top of the pool (formal or informal), on which to grow plants that need their roots permanently submerged. It is easily made.

Bring the cement walls and the wooden framework to within about 9 inches of the surface of the ground, then excavate more soil to form the shelf (Fig. 6) behind the main walls; dig down far enough to provide a ridge to keep the soil on the shelf from being washed into the pool.

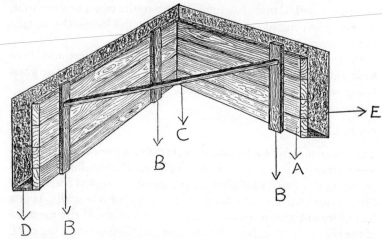

Fig. 5. Shows cutaway section of wooden framework erected for
construction of formal pool

A = horizontal boards   C = wooden braces
B = strong upright posts   D = space to be filled with concrete
                 E = soil

The shelf can be made as wide as you wish. The short
retaining wall at the back can be built of bricks or of cement,
in which case you will need a narrow wooden support to hold
the lining till it hardens.

Soil is placed on the shelf; and when the pool is filled, the
water naturally flows over into it. (See Fig. 6.)

As regards draining the pool: like some builders, you may not
bother about laying special pipes and prefer to use the method
described for the informal pool, viz. change the water slowly by
means of a hose-pipe and a fine spray of tap-water. Or install a
pump – used also to supply a fountain jet – in the pool.

Normally, however, a drainage-pipe leading to a sump, is
laid at the bottom before the sides are lined. The most efficient
is the stop-cock type operated by a long-arm key (removable of
course and used when required). The apparatus is contained in
a vertical brick chamber built on to the side of the pool, and
the chamber hidden by a lid of some sort, preferably a stone
slab.

The outlet hole, through which the stagnant water is to pass
is protected from the soil on the bottom of the pool by a brickwork ridge (one or two layers of bricks) built along the side.

And the hole itself is covered with a piece of perforated zinc to keep the debris or the fish from entering the pipe. (See Fig. 6.)

Although the handyman will find the job simple, the average gardener would no doubt prefer to call in an expert to install the apparatus.

For a small ornamental pool (such as most of us will build) an ordinary lead pipe can be fitted just over the soil bed and plugged with a stopper or a cork of some sort which is easy to remove by hand when the water has to be drained off. Another method – the most simple – is to use a bottle with the bottom knocked out (an old-fashioned stone hot-water bottle is excellent). Cement it in position, fixing the broken end in an ordinary drainage pipe. The screwtop to the bottle is easily removed when necessary and the water flows into a soakaway about 3 feet from the pool.

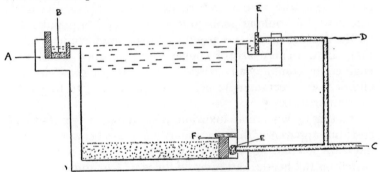

Fig. 6. Shows details in construction of formal pool

A = concrete lining   D = overflow pipe
B = soil on shelf   E = perforated zinc
C = drainage pipe   F = brickwork ridge covered with slate

The soakaway or pit should of course be big enough to absorb all the water. But if the soil is light and sandy, it will take any amount.

For a small pool dig out the existing soil to a depth of 3 feet (a foot deeper than the pool); the end of the pipe will thus appear in the pit a foot above the bottom. Fill the pit – the 12 inches below the pipe and the 2 feet above – with clinkers and cinders; put some soil on top and some grass turves to give a neat finish to the job.

If an overflow-pipe is required, it should be installed at the same time as the drainage pipe and is best connected to it. (See

Fig. 6.) Fine mesh wire must be placed over the exit point, otherwise floating material will be washed into the pipe.

Swimming pools will require a different system of draining: a pump is often used or pipes are laid leading to the main drains of the house.

A swimming-pool may be too ambitious an undertaking for the part-time or the week-end gardener and is best left to the specialist. One of the most up-to-date and efficient types is that built by the 'Gunite' method (see page 87). It is apparently the popular type of swimming-pool in the U.S.A. and according to one firm about a million of these pools have been built there between 1952 and 1963. By this method the excavated areas is reinforced with steel ribbing and the walls and the floor sprayed with concrete under pressure. The completed pool is all one piece, leakproof and immensely strong. Another great advantage is that the actual construction takes only a few days. The cost of an oblong pool, 30 feet by 15 feet – a popular size for the average family – is around £1,600, and includes a filtration plant. (There are of course much cheaper kinds. One engineering company advertises them in three shapes – circular, elliptical and rectangular; prices ranging from £10 to £1,000 for standard sizes.)

Heating makes a more luxurious pool; it naturally adds to the cost; but apparently the vast majority of pools being built these days are heated. So you can swim all the year round. Just switch on the heater and jump in for your Christmas dip!

Luxury swimming-pools are fairly expensive, but many firms have an extended payment system which most purchasers take advantage of.

Ordinary immersion heaters are sometimes used for small outdoor ornamental pools in which tropical Water-lilies are grown. The pool must be reasonably near an electric supply point. Such a pool can also be stocked with some of the beautifully coloured tropical fish, provided one can keep the temperature constant.

INDOOR POOLS AND TANKS

Greenhouse pools for tropical aquatics and tropical fish are made in the same way as the outdoor pool. Circular pools of stone slightly raised above the floor have a more harmonious

22

Miscanthus sacchariflorus. Long leaves with a prominent white mid-rib grows to a height of 6 feet.

23
Formal pool in
the Italian style.

—*Photo H. Smith*

appearance indoors than the square or the oblong; and if about 2 feet high, are more accessible – moreover it is pleasant to be able to sit on the edge and look down comfortably at the plants and the fish.

The building is best done by an expert, since some sort of heating apparatus usually has to be installed. The thermostatic control method is by far the best in my opinion and although rather expensive is the most reliable.

It is sometimes possible to get fine old lead cisterns with carved work in relief, or stone basin-like receptacles, both of which can be used as miniature standing pools in a hot-house. I've seen them in the Brompton Road, Chelsea (where they are certainly expensive) and also in some markets where you can often pick up something suitable quite cheap. The rectangular lead cistern is seen to best advantage stood flush with a wall. Round containers, on the other hand, should be stood about the floor.

Wooden tubs are the cheapest but not always easy to get nowadays. In the past it was possible to buy an old oyster-tub from the fishmonger; but I have not seen many of them recently. They are about 12 inches in diameter and 9 inches deep: a useful size for a small Water-lily and a couple of goldfish. Out of doors they should be sunk in the ground. An empty beer barrel cut down to a reasonable depth also makes an ideal receptacle for an outdoor pool.

I have frequently seen the fragrant blue-flowered tropical

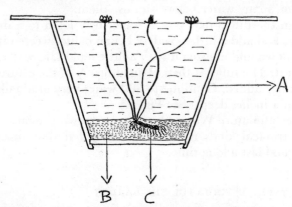

Fig. 7. Shows section of tub pool with Water-lily tuber planted in loam

A = wooden tub   B = loam   C = tuber

D

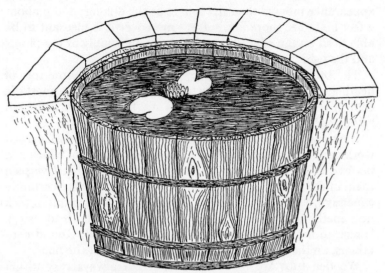

Fig. 8. Shows wooden tub pool sunk in the ground, with a surround of paving stones

Water-lily DAUBENYANA growing well in an oyster-tub in a hot-house (see under Var. DAUBENYANA. The leaves are floating and an excellent foil to the charming blue flowers.

These tubs, made of good solid oak, are usually quite clean and ready for use. However, it is wise to give them a good scrub with hot, soapy water before you use them.

When the tub is dry, put in some turfy loam to a depth of 4 inches and add a little powdered charcoal to sweeten it; press it well down and moisten it with a little tepid rain water, if you can get it. The tuber is then planted firmly in the centre and a little water added. Continue to add water very gradually till it is about 4 inches deep. (See Fig. 7.)

Other miniature Water-lilies can be grown similarly. Many of the tropical kinds make delightful cut flowers during the winter and last a long time.

OTHER TYPES OF POOLS FOR THE GARDEN

Pools made of carved stone blocks or of marble are indubitably the finest and most beautiful. They are mostly designed as fountain-pools and many are found in old Italian gardens. The

raised marble pool at the Villa Pia in the Vatican Gardens
(built for Pope Pius IV, 1560) is a magnificent example. The
main fountain rises from a raised basin in the middle of the
pool; smaller jets, 12 inches high, are set in the main basin
opposite each other. The rim is rounded and carved and gives a
perfect finish to the pool; and the water is clear and shallow
and contains neither plants nor fish. (See Fig. 9.)

Fig. 9. Formal marble or stone pool

Pools made of stone or marble can be of any depth, since
they are built in sections. For the ordinary concrete pool you
excavate soil to whatever depth you wish: 6 feet, if you like.
But for the pre-fabricated ones – in fibre-glass, for instance –
you are spared the labour of deep digging: you need only sink
the pool in a depression half its depth, piling and packing the
soil you remove round the sides. Its irregular shape (the usual
shape) makes the pool ideally suited to an informal setting: it
can be sunk in a rock-garden or against a grass slope. The one
disadvantage is that all these ready-made pools are shallow –
seldom more than 18 inches in depth. It is impossible therefore
to grow any of those glorious Water-lilies that need deep water,
say, 3 feet or more. Another point: these pools have no drainage
or overflow apparatus and it will be necessary to change the

water (if you wish to) by ladling it out. Many specialists, however, maintain that it is unnecessary to empty a pool, that fish
and certain oxygenating plants will keep the water clean and
clear. Rain also helps and along with fish and aquatics will
eventually refresh the water in any type of pool.*

These pre-fabricated pools (moulded in tough resin-bonded
glass-fibre) last a life-time. When preparing the ground, where
they are to be sunk, all sharp-pointed stones and flints, however,
must be removed; for in time they may penetrate the base and
do irreparable damage.

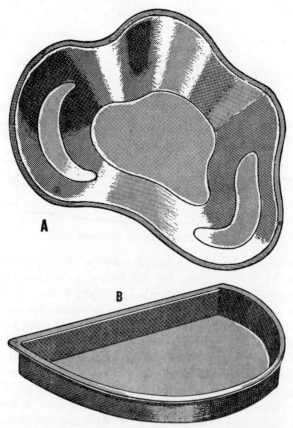

Fig. 10. Showing different kinds of fibre-glass shapes for Garden-Pools

* You can buy Water Clarifiers from chemists and horticultural stores.
CLAROX clears the cloudiest water and destroys all algae.

There is a large variety of shapes available, prices ranging from about £7 10s. to £50. The most expensive I've seen so far is an elegant rectangular one, 8 feet 5 inches in length, 5 feet 5 inches across and 18 inches deep. It holds roughly 250 gallons of water. It has a ledge about 12 inches wide round the entire perimeter, on which to grow marginal plants; and it is ideal for the small formal garden. Its cost is about £48.

One of the biggest of the irregular-shaped types (roughly heart-shaped) holds about 220 gallons. Its open water surface is an area of 32 square feet. The moulding provides for different depths: a shelf along the side of the pool for shallow-rooting aquatics and deeper shelves or ledges farther in for Water-lilies.

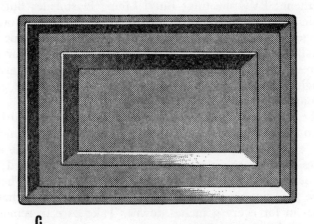

C

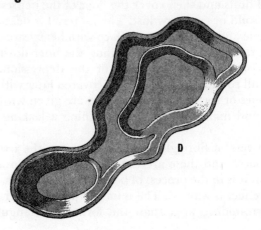

D

The smallest of the formal pre-fabricated pools is a circular one 4 feet 10 inches across and 7 inches deep – rather like a giant soup-plate. It holds 50 gallons. Another is semicircular (half the size of the preceding pool – actually the shape halved). The straight edge at the back makes the pool ideal for setting at the base of a low wall in a formal garden. It is similar in shape to the old stone semicircular sinks that one sometimes comes across in gardens. (See Fig. 10B.) With these sinks, the stone-work at the edge (rounded and mellowed, covered with moss and lichen) is left exposed; the fibre-glass shapes, however, should have their edges covered with grass or effectually disguised with pebbles and small stones. (See Fig. 10 A, B, C, D.)

There are other materials (literally materials) for garden pools. Polythene; PVC sheeting; Butyl Liner; Plastolene; Butalene; Juralene; all obtainable in the size required – some, however, stronger than others. I have recently seen a pool-shape lined with Butyl Pool Liner – it is obtainable in one colour only: Charcoal (grey-black), which looks natural against grass; I thought it most effective. The cost is 24s. per running foot, the standard width being 13 feet.

The method of laying these materials is simple. Soil is dug out to form the shape of the pool required. Usually 24 inches is deep enough for a biggish pool. A shelf 9 inches wide and 9 inches from the top is made as the soil is being removed; on it will be stood suitable marginal plants in containers. The sides of the pool slope gradually, at an angle of about 30° (that is, 2 inches in for every 3 inches down). Take care to remove all stones and flints and then cover the floor of the depression with fine sand, soild or even sawdust. The material is next stretched over the hole and loosely held in place with heavy stones. Water is run in gradually, the weight pulling the liner down till it is moulded completely to the shape of the depression. A neat flap is left all round the surface to be covered later with suitable edging stones or rocks. Full instructions are given with all these materials and many are suitable for lining a leaking concrete pool.

Most buyers of fibre-glass pools plump for the irregular or informal ones. And these are the easiest to place in a garden, especially if it is in the process of being planned and a free or a semi-wild effect is wanted. The informal pool is easier to marry to the surrounding area than the formal, rectangular type, which needs an appropriate lay-out: usually immediately sur-rounding it and enclosing it are good quality flagstones laid close together and forming wide walks or pathways edged with perhaps a low wall of sandstone blocks or slabs or a clipped hedge. Often at the end of the formal garden facing the pool is a stone seat or a small summer-house, which provides a focal point and often serves to emphasize the spaciousness of the lay-out and the classical lines of the design. (See illustration.)

The informal pool, on the other hand, is much easier to place. Its immediate surroundings should be free and unadorned. Nevertheless statues are sometimes set up on the banks of these pools. The life-size figure sitting gazing into the pool at Midelney Place, Somerset, is very effective, though a little startling to come across in the fading light of a summer evening! (See page 116.) Informal pools are best surrounded by grass and suitable water-side plants. And, to save the grass from being worn down, roughly-shaped paving-stones (about 9 inches square) are, as a rule, laid round the edge. You walk on them if you like – it is all free and easy.

If the surrounding ground slopes up from the pool, it is important that it should be grassed, otherwise dirt and impuri-ties get washed down in the water and may do a lot of harm.

Rushes, Reeds, a few hardy Primulas, perhaps – nothing too tall – may be planted near the edge. No Willows, for example, should be grown anywhere near; these are all right in the back-ground, especially where a large pool has been sunk; but for the small and medium-sized informal pool, low-growing things like dwarf Japanese Maples, slow-growing evergreens and Heather are the best choice.

Tubs and half-barrels are ideal for the rock-garden. Half a barrel (about 20 inches high) makes a good pool for a restricted space. It should be made from an old beer or wine barrel and scrubbed clean. It is sunk into the ground, the top coming about 3 inches below the surface; flat stone slabs are then arranged round it to conceal the wood. See Fig. 8. These miniature pools can be set close to boulders or vertical rocks, which have trailing Alpines growing over them.

In the tub plant one of the LAYDEKERI pygmy Water-lilies and an oxygenating plant or two, if there is room; the Water Buttercup (*Ranunculus aquatilis*) is recommended by aquarists, but is invasive and may have to be divided up rather frequently.

Goldfish add to the beauty of pools. The common sort (*Carassius auratus*) came originally from China and is one of the loveliest and the most popular; it is completely hardy and thrives well in quite shallow water.

As regards repairing tubs and barrels: cracks in the sides should be filled with a heavy, stiff clay, which soon hardens and makes the tub leakproof.

The large circular pool, 10 or 12 feet across, such as the one at Cliveden, with its fountain and elaborate statuary, obviously requires a formal setting. It is well placed there, standing at the end of a long drive facing the north front of the house. And the pool at Knightshayes Court, Devon, is surrounded by a wide expanse of lawn, bounded by clipped Yew hedges. The lay-out is a magnificent example of classical simplicity.

CHAPTER EIGHT

Planting and Decorating

M<small>ANY</small> of the plants which are grown on the banks of a river or a stream are equally suitable for a pool. One important thing to remember, however, is that for the average-sized garden pool they should be on the small side. And for a tub they must be miniatures. The tall *Iris sibirica*, for instance, would look top-heavy close to a tiny pool. We are limited in our choice to dwarf species such as *Iris cristata* and *I. douglasiana*. There are plenty of them.

These waterside plants are often called marginal plants and certain kinds are sometimes set *in* the water of large pools – on shelves or ledges.

Iris pumila is a charming little species and the best known and toughest of all the dwarf kinds. It is about 4 inches high with small tufts of sword-like leaves and flowers about 2 inches deep carried singly on very short stems. The variety CAEURLEA is prized by gardeners for the exquisite blue colour of its flowers. Var. ATTICA has pale straw yellow flowers tinged with green, with a brownish spot on the petals; and EXCELSA is another charming yellow variety.

These pretty little plants need a well-drained soil containing lime and they like full sun. They are ideal for growing by those miniature artificial pools – tubs, half-barrels and other receptacles – which are sunk into the ground. In time the plants spread and make clumps which should be divided up every so often; the rhizomes must be partly exposed on the soil. The amount of water which may overflow from a tiny pool will do them no harm; it will be quickly absorbed and help to mellow the ground.

Iris pumila and its many varieties are not suitable for riverside planting or for moist, boggy situations. The plants bloom in April and are natives of Europe and Asia Minor.

I. cristata is about 6 inches high with small flowers, lilac and yellow in colour, and narrow leaves. It is one of the dwarf species that likes plenty of moisture in summer; but it should be lifted in the autumn and its fleshy roots must be stored in sand till March and then replanted. It blooms in May.

Two other species suitable for growing on the edge of a small pool are *I. douglasiana* (9 inches), a dwarf from California, with narrow leaves and flowers, usually bluish, with golden yellow lines; and *I. setosa*, a very variable species, sometimes 6 inches high, sometimes 2 feet; its colouring varies enormously too; usually it is an attractive lilac-purple shade. Most nurseries stock the plant and describe it as having 'Lilac-purple flowers; a striking dwarf compact plant for moist soil.'

With the exception of *I. pumila*, which is really a rock-garden type, these Irises need damp situations but will not tolerate stagnant moisture.

For large pools the following kinds are some of the best; though one must not plant too many – usually a single clump of one kind is enough. *Iris sibirica* (3 to 4 feet); *I. graminea*, reddish-blue and violet – scented (1½ feet); *I. aurea*, golden-yellow; a strong grower (4 feet); *I. ochroleuca* Var. QUEEN VICTORIA, creamy-white with an orange blotch (5 feet); *I. delavayi*, deep violet (5 feet).

For ledges or shelves in large pools *Iris laevigata* and the famous *I. kaempferi* should be chosen. (See page 30.) They flourish luxuriantly in shallow water. The rhizomes of the latter, however, should be above water-level during the winter.

I am of the opinion that a well-designed pool, especially the formal circular pool, is sufficient in itself and that too lavish a use of brightly coloured flowers detracts from the quiet beauty of the water. Actually, I have seen some pools so overplanted that no water was visible!

Do not plant too many flowers, then, even round a large pool. A few suggestions. Try a single clump of purple *Iris kaempferi* on a shallow ledge in the water; or a clump or a drift of yellow *Primula florindae* in the shadiest part of the pool. They, too, will grow in very shallow water during the summer. Have a clump outside the pool and a smaller one in the water. Or use the brilliant red Astilbe called FANAL in the same way. (See page 27.) The soft feathery plumes (2 feet high) are very effective reflected in the water.

Do not plant the three together, for they bloom simultaneously and in full bloom would produce a garish effect. Round a good-sized pool they should be spaced well apart and suitable foliage-plants such as Reeds, Rushes or moisture-loving Ferns interposed between them.

There are plenty of beautiful flowers suitable for planting at the edge of an informal pool. It is a pity we can grow only a few, but it is essential if a natural effect is wanted.

The double Kingcup or Marsh Marigold (*Caltha palustris* var. *plena*), with its golden-yellow flowers, does best at water-level. It is about 9 inches tall and a single clump is enough for a tiny pool, perhaps situated in the rock-garden.

It needs a deep rich loamy soil which is always moist. The flowers are at their best in May. It looks well on its own; let it come up to the edge of the water and let the grass grow fairly close round it.

Irises have been mentioned already and also many of the moisture-loving Primulas. The latter, unfortunately, require deep shade during the sunniest part of the day; and there is often very little near an open pool; but they don't mind the sun so much when their roots are in water.

The cinnamon-scented *Primula sikkimensis*, 18 inches tall, is one of the best. The flowers are like large Cowslips and a pretty shade of yellow. It flourishes luxuriantly in a little water and will seed itself freely in moist soils.

Ranunculus are related to *Caltha*. Some are grown in the water as oxygenating plants (*Ranunculus aquatilis*, for instance). Some species need moist or wet soils. Some are grown in the water as floating plants. And a large number are suitable for planting in the herbaceous border.

R. bullatus grows 9 inches high and has attractive, fragrant orange-coloured flowers, rather like those of a large Kingcup. It is particularly useful for a pool, since it revels in full sun, but is a poor plant in cold, exposed gardens.

R. lingua (indigenous to Britain) is another lovely waterside plant. It is like a tall Buttercup (2 or 3 feet high as a rule) and has narrow, lance-shaped leaves and open shining yellow flowers which bloom from June to September. Its roots are densely fibrous and like damp, marshy soils. It is hardier than *R. bullatus*. These Ranunculas are usually raised from seeds sown in spring. (Most of the other kinds thrive in good deep loams.)

Trollius belong to the same family and have large, round, buttercup-like flowers, globe-shaped – they are often called Globe Flowers. One of the best-known species is *Trollius europaeus*, a native plant (more common in cooler northern regions than in the south), with erect branched stems carrying citron-yellow flowers and beautifully divided dark green leaves. The plant is 18 inches to 2 feet high and needs a rich moist loam.

There are some excellent garden forms derived from *T. hybridus*: one of the loveliest is SPRINGHILL BEAUTY with lovely orange-yellow flowers which bloom in May. The plant is about 2 feet high. It may be increased by division of the roots in spring. I am always a little apprehensive, however, of this method of propagating Trollius, since the plants so easily deteriorate after splitting up. It is often best to get new specimens of any variety one is particularly fond of; and as regards the species, to raise them from seed, which should be sown in loamy, well dug soil where the plants are to bloom.

HARDY ORNAMENTAL GRASSES

Various kinds of ornamental Grasses and Rushes are found wild in Britain. Some grow by lakes and rivers and in damp marshy places – several on the seashore – and the best of them are often cut and dried for winter decoration indoors. The Bulrush and the Reed Mace are two of the finest; and the kinds we find by the riverside are usually too tall and grow too big for a garden pool. (They are described on pages 41–42.) These 6-foot Reeds are difficult to accommodate in most gardens; but there are smaller species which are excellent for associating with waterside flowers. And on the whole they look more natural there than many of the flowers; ideally these Reeds should be used as oil-plants: set near tall things like the Candelabra Primulas; and they do best with their roots in water. Plant one or two clumps, depending on the size of the pool, on a ledge in the water. *Scirpus tabernaemontanus zebrinus* is one of the smaller Bulrushes, often about 18 inches tall, but sometimes taller. Specimens I have seen in gardens around London have been about 2 feet and grew in smallish pools. The stems are marked transversely with white and green and look very striking by the waterside. The plant prospers in a shallow pool. This ornamental Rush is a native of Japan.

Typha are rampant aquatic Grasses which soon get out of control and need to be contained in a box or a plastic planting-crate to keep them from spreading out into the pool. There is a delightful miniature, viz. *Typha minima*, which grows about 12 inches high and is an excellent margin plant. It has narrow, rush-like leaves and tiny brownish flower-heads – the typical flower-spike of many Rushes.

Typha laxmanni is a medium-sized species with slender stems not more than about 4 feet tall – sometimes half that. The leaves are narrow, ¼ inch wide; and the flower-spike is rusty brown. It is a fine waterside plant and an excellent foil to some of the deep pink Candelabra Primulas.

An attractive yellow Ornamental Grass is *Alopecurus pratensia* Var. AUREUS. It is known as the Meadow Foxtail Grass, the spike resembling the form of a soft, furry tail. This lovely foliage-plant is often used for formal bedding and does well in ordinary soils. It flourishes most luxuriantly, however, in rich, moist ground and is therefore valuable for growing on the edge of a pool. It is sometimes listed in catalogues under *Var. foliis variegatis* and described as: 'A pretty form of the Meadow Foxtail Grass with tufts of narrow leaves, striped straw-yellow – 1 to 3 feet high.' The type plant (*A. pratensis*) is a native of Britain.

Carex morrowii variegata is a dwarf Sedge (a rush-like plant) which isn't hardy in all districts and is often grown in a pot for indoor decoration. It is a fine waterside plant in southern gardens and reaches about 1 foot in height. The leaves are stiff, evergreen, long-pointed, with a white line near each margin. This species is probably the most decorative of all the Carex and the only one offered by nurseries; it costs about 3s. 6d. a plant.

Dactylis glomerata elegantissima is commonly known as the Cock's-foot Grass (so named from the appearance of its large, distantly-spaced three-branched panicle). It is among the most attractive of the hardy Ornamental Grasses we grow in our gardens – of slender habit, about 12 inches high and forms dense tufts of grey-green leaves. You often see it used as a foliage-plant in formal beds and it is equally decorative by the edge of a pool. It can be obtained from most nurseries and is quite expensive, costing about 5s. 6d. a root. However, like most of these Grasses, it is easily increased by dividing the plants in spring or autumn. Or it can be raised from seed. Sow the seeds where they are to grow in March or April.

Elymus arenarius is a fairly tall plant, often reaching a height of 4 feet and carrying attractive blue-green spikes about 4 inches long. Its common name is Lyme Grass (*Lyme* is an old form of *lime*), and the plant is used widely on the Continent for fixing sea-sands. S. Thompson described it in his book *Wild Flowers*, published in 1854: 'The Lyme Grass (*Elymus*) by binding the sands with its roots, assists in the resistance to the encroachments of the sea.' It flourishes in damp, sandy soil; but as it spreads so quickly, it should be planted only by the largest pools and will have to be dug up and thinned out every second year. Hilliers stock it (3s. a plant) and describe it as 'A strong-growing, beautifully glaucous-leaved Grass. . ."

Festuca ovina glauca is probably the best known of all the Ornamental Grasses. It is frequently used as a foliage-plant in the herbaceous border, and its lovely bluish colour makes it a favourite edging plant for formal flower-beds. (It looks singularly attractive used as an underplanting to the tall Regale Lilies.) This bluish spiky Grass is one of the most suitable for planting in a clump by the side of a small pool. It thrives in practically any soil, though it prefers cool situations. *Festuca* is easily increased by division; small sections with a root or roots attached should be planted out where the plants are to grow permanently.

Glyceria belongs to the Gramineae Family as does *Festuca*. *Glyceria aquatica variegata* is the most attractive of the species for the garden and grows about 18 inches tall. It is an excellent Ornamental Grass for a small pool and decorative enough there on its own.

The leaves, an inch wide, are striped with white; and the green-and-white effect is especially beautiful when seen in semi-shade or in the subdued light of the evening. In spring and autumn the foliage is tinted pink. As the plant is inclined to be invasive, it should be grown in a container near the water, or thinned out every second year. This Grass costs about 3s. 6d. a plant.

Holcus mollis variegatus, known as the Variegated Soft Grass, is a woolly plant, dwarf and tufted, 6 to 9 inches tall – very useful for a limited space. The striking silver variegation in the leaves makes it an ideal little plant for growing in a single clump near a miniature pool.

Stipa pennata is the Feather Grass – which has graceful, feather-like spikes or plumes. It is densely tufted, the stems 2 feet tall, the leaves green and narrow and the spikelets measure about ½ inch long. Many people grow it to use in making dry bouquets, and it is one of the loveliest of Grasses for the water-side. Like the other species described above, it may be increased by division in March, or by seeds sown outside in April.

HARDY FERNS

(See chapter 1, pages 28–29, for a descriptive list of some of the best of these.) None of the Ornamental Grasses grow in water, nor do they need excessive moisture for their well-being. And they all thrive in full sun. Hardy Ferns, on the other hand, need shady places and plenty of moisture; and there are quite a number that will grow in water or at least with their roots spreading out and reaching it. The Royal Fern, *Osmunda regalis*, for instance, prospers exceedingly in wet places, so do the Ostrich Fern and the Sensitive Fern. It might be thought, then, that Ferns are difficult to accommodate near a pool in a sunny spot. Lack of shade may be partly compensated for by a deep moist soil; and if the Ferns are set in the water, perhaps on a shallow ledge, they will do very well. Another method is to grow them in the type of Bog-garden described in the following chapter.

Adiantum pedatum is the Hardy Maidenhair Fern, a native of North America, Japan, China and the Himalayas. The delicate, airy green fronds ere carried on shining, black stems 18 inches or so in height. It is recommended by many gardeners for growing in conjunction with the hardy Cypripediums (Orchids), which like Bog-gardens and similar places. (See page 123.) The Maidenhair-like foliage is an excellent foil to these rare, lovely plants and also to Primulas and Polyanthuses. It prefers a shady spot and according to some growers is less hardy than many of our other garden Ferns. In cold districts it should be given a sheltered spot – perhaps set against a rock by the side of a pool – and it needs a deep moist soil made up of one part each of chopped peat, garden loam, silver sand and sifted leafmould. A good time for planting is early October. The soil should not be packed too tightly round the roots. (Use the same mixture for the other hardy Ferns and plant them also in early autumn, if you can.)

Blechnum spicant. See pages 27 and 28.

Blechnum tabulare is a large-leaved evergreen Fern, with leathery, dark green fronds which form wide clumps 2 feet high. (Good specimens may be seen in the Savill Gardens at Windsor.) But it is not hardy in all gardens and should be given a sheltered place in districts north of London. It likes plenty of moisture and could be grown on the edge of a pool in a wild garden where there is a swampy or boggy place. Hillier offers it at 7s. 6d. a plant and describes it as 'A very handsome, evergreen large-leaved fern. Fronds leathery and dark green.'

Ceterach officinarum will thrive in a crevice of a wall; it could be used where a pool has a bricked edge or surround, and planted between the bricks on the shadiest side. It is a dwarf species from 4 to 6 inches high, and must be kept well watered during the summer months. Most gardeners grow it in loam, lime-rubble, rock chippings and sand. It is a perfect little Fern for planting in cascades, where it can catch the spray of the falling water. A native of Britain, Europe, Northern Asia. Its common name is Rusty-back Fern.

Dryopteris filix-mas. See page 28.

Dryopteris thelypteris is a favourite species for growing in Water-gardens, and usually about the beginning of May you can see its fresh, lacy, green leaves appearing above the ground. It likes a damp, black leafmould, and when fully grown has fronds a foot tall and 4 inches wide – often they are larger. It will thrive in a sunny spot, provided it gets ample moisture all through the growing season. It is found wild in many parts of the world including Britain. As a background plant to a clump of yellow *Primula sikkimensis* it is superb.

The Ostrich Fern referred to above is *Matteucia struthiopteris*. It is the biggest of our hardy Ferns and likes a moist shady position in the Water-garden. It could be grown in the Bog-garden, since it needs water at its roots the year round and would make an excellent background for tall Primulas growing on the margin of a pool. The large graceful fronds are plume-like or feather-like and produce a very pleasing effect when massed in the Water-garden. Hillier calls it: 'The largest and handsomest of European Ferns: 3 to 5 feet.' It is one of the expensive kinds, costing 7s. 6d. a plant.

For the Royal Fern (*Osmunda regalis*) see page 28.

Onoclea sensibilis is a most useful plant for the edge of a pool, for it needs moisture at its roots all through the year and it likes sunny places. It reaches a height of 12 inches and spreads rapidly in the peaty, leafy soils in which it grows. The young foliage is unfortunately often damaged by frost, hence its common name: Sensitive Fern.

The Hart's-tongue Fern is one of our most common wildings and may often be found growing in the crevices of old stone walls and at the foot of boulders in rocky places. It will grow in most shady gardens where there is some moist light sandy, leafy soil. The best mixture consists of sifted leafmould, loam and silver sand in equal parts. There are many very attractive varieties, all evergreen and therefore useful as foliage-plants through the winter months. The type plant *Phyllitis scolopendrium*, with its simple, strap-shaped deep green fronds, is sometimes used in the stone surround of a formal pool, quite low down near the water; it is best set in position when the sides or the top part is being built. The plants should be watered very freely during a dry spell. The variety CRISPUM GRANDE has beautifully waved fronds. Planting is best done in April or October and if the Ferns grow where the sun catches them during the day, they should be well soaked regularly in April and then mulched with a good depth of leaf-mould. There is an enormous number of different varieties, all very attractive garden plants and all flourishing luxuriantly near water.

Polystichum setigerum, with fronds 2 feet high, is a beautiful evergreen Fern which likes a certain amount of sun. It is a fine foliage-plant for the edge of a pool where its roots can reach the water and a good foil-plant to some of the tall-growing moisture-loving Irises and Primulas. It is found in all parts of the world including Britain and is commonly known as the Soft Shield Fern.

Hardy Ferns grown in the garden like a good, deep, moist root-run and given that will tolerate a certain amount of sun.

They are easily propagated by division; the plants are lifted in April, carefully divided up into pieces, each piece having a frond and a portion of the rhizome with roots attached.

For a small pool some of the dwarfer evergreen kinds are most valuable, since they can provide attractive foliage effects all through the winter in a very limited space.

OXYGENATING PLANTS

People who keep fish in their ponds are more interested in these plants than those who grow only Water-lilies and similar aquatics. Oxygenating or submerged plants, as they are sometimes called, are necessary in the aquarium to provide food and oxygen for fish and other animal life. And there are other reasons for growing them. In an indoor aquarium many are pleasant to look at – graceful, airy, underwater plants seen through the glass. Some kinds are used for testing the water, to discover whether it is fit for fish to live in: *Nitella* is one of these: if it lives, so will the fish. Other kinds absorb the waste products given off by fish and they also inhibit the growth of algae (a floating cloudy green organism), which is starved out by the larger, stronger-growing oxygenating plants

Anacharis canadensis is recommended by nurseries as 'an oxygenator and for giving shelter to fish.' This is a native of North America, and despite its recommendation by the experts, should be kept for an aquarium where it can be easily controlled. Outside in a pool or in a stream it is something of a menace, spreading rapidly and choking everything near it. It flowers rarely, and its leaves, dark green, come in great abundance on branching, brittle stems. No cultivation is necessary: a few shoots can be dropped into the water where they will grow beneath the surface and make long, slender leafy stems. Its common name is Canadian Pond Weed. It is sold by the bunch: the cost is 2s. a bunch.

The species *A. crispa*, a very leafy plant, is less rampant. The stems are densely clothed with narrow, reflexed leaves. It is planted in sandy soil at the bottom of a shallow pool or a tank.

Callitriche verna, the Water Starwort, has dense tufts of bright green leaves; these are submerged at first and then rise to the surface during the summer. They afford excellent shade for fish and water insects. And the plant is listed in catalogues as a 'really good oxygenator.' Like the Canadian Pond Weed, however, it is extremely invasive in pools and best in a cold water aquarium.

Ceratophyllum demersum is planted like *Anacharis canadensis*; the small pieces rooting and floating in the water. The plants make densely-branched stems with narrow whorled leaves, dark green in colour. Hillier offers it and describes it as a first-class oxygenator suitable for soil-less ponds.

Hottonia palustris is the Water Violet, a charming aquatic with loose spikes of mauvish flowers. The finely divided leaves are submerged and the flowers are carried on leafless stems well above the water and bloom in early summer. The *Hottonia* have creeping rootstocks. These are planted in April in wet soil on the margins of pools or on a shallow ledge. The plant is a native of Europe and found in some of our ponds and rivulets.

Potamogeton crispus, called the Curled Pondweed because of the wavy-edged leaves (3 inches long and ½ inch wide). These are a brownish-red in full sunlight and give a pretty glowing effect in summer, when the sun shines through them.

Ranunculus aquatilis (mentioned on page 103) has both floating and submerged leaves. The former are 3-lobed and dark green; the latter are divided into thread-like segments. The snow-white flowers come in spring and resemble miniature Water-lilies. A good oxygenator but very invasive.

Oxygenating plants are often set in containers, and in this way are more easily controlled. The containers may be had in various sizes; the largest will take as many as fifteen plants.

FLOATING PLANTS

Water-lilies are floating plants and the most beautiful of all of them, though aquarists state they have little value, apart from providing shade in the breeding pool during the summer months. In the outside pool they serve a purpose, then, where there are goldfish; but it is for their glorious flowers of course that they are principally grown.

The genuine floating plants, such as those described below, are necessary to help control algae and to provide food for fish. One plant or a portion of a plant to every 10 square feet of water is recommended.

Aponogeton distachyus, the Water Hawthorn, a native of the Cape of Good Hope, has become naturalized in some parts of southern England. It has floating leaves and in summer white, fragrant flowers, which often bloom intermittently through the year. The roots of about three plants should be set in loamy soil in a wire basket or a plastic container and sunk to the bottom of a pool, the depth of water being about 2 feet. The plant spreads rapidly and must be controlled.

Azolla caroliniana. (See page 89.) This is a miniature floating

plant and, like the preceding, has become naturalized in
Britain. It is closely allied to the Ferns and increases alarmingly
by natural division. It soon covers a pool or a stream with green
foliage, and the delicate fern-like foliage is extremely attractive.
The popular name of the plant is Fairy Moss.

Hydrocharis morus-ranae has small bright green leaves which
float on the water and tiny, three-petalled white flowers. It
spreads rapidly like many floating and oxygenating aquatics;
and the method of growing it is simply to lay a plant on the
water. It is propagated by division in summer.

Lemna trisulca is called the Ivy-leaved Duckweed, and has pale
green leaf-like fronds ½ inch long which in summer float grace-
fully on the surface of a pool and provide shade for fish; it also
helps to keep the water clear.

Stratiotes aloides is a native plant which remains below the
water for best part of the year, and rises when it is ready to
flower. The flowers are snow-white, and the leaves, star-shaped
and spiky, come in rosettes. The common name is Water
Soldier.

These are but a few of the oxygenating and floating plants
that can be obtained from nurseries. They are less important in
pools where there are no fish, and are not required, of course, in
formal pools where nothing is grown.

Large circular pools are nearly always treated as formal pools
and left unadorned, like the one at Knightshayes Court, Devon.
(See page 104.) Often they have a simple surround of flagstones
and are set in the middle of a wide expanse of well-mown grass.
Some have a simple fountain or a few Water-lilies floating on
the water. Many, however, have neither ornaments nor plants;
and there is something truly satisfying about the still water with
nothing to break the surface except the wind and the rain.

Story's circular pool at Cliveden has a sumptuous fountain in
the middle, with nude figures in a giant cockleshell, and low
down near the water are one or two clumps of Bamboos. It
stands at the end of the north avenue, facing the house. Tall
evergreen trees make an ideal background.*

Formal pools are wasted in the wild garden; for shape is
unimportant there, the waterside plants, first encroaching, and

* Story, William Wetmore, American poet and sculptor, settled in Rome.
(1819–1895.)

finally covering and hiding the outline completely. Although no symmetrical shape is required, the round or roundish pool is a good choice. It sits there easily among Rushes, Reeds and other aquatics.

There is unfortunately often a tendency to overplant, shrubs and moisture-loving plants covering almost every square inch of the surrounding ground. One can learn a great deal about planting and decorating pools by visiting those gardens where the lay-outs have been planned by professional gardeners.

Midelney Place in Somerset has a very beautiful Water-garden (mentioned in the previous chapter), the motif being a large roundish informal pool. (See page 103.) It is partly enclosed by shrubs, with a background of taller trees. The edge is grassed to provide a walk, and Reeds and Rushes grow in and near the water. The life-size statue of a naked youth sitting staring into the water is thought to be out of place by some visitors. ('Enough to frighten anybody to death!' according to one lady.) However, many people like to see statues and other ornaments placed near water. Personally I think they are more suitable for decorating a formal pool than for setting among waterside plants in a wild garden.

Our so-called Japanese Gardens are a curious mixture of water, bridges, stone lanterns and various other eastern orna-ments. Dwarfed trees, ornamental flowering Cherry-trees and rockwork are also used. Many are confined to rather small areas and are inclined to look overcrowded. They need careful plan-ning and are best treated as special features of the garden proper. Information on making and planting a Japanese Water-garden is given in chapter 11.

CHAPTER NINE

Making a Bog-Garden

THERE are many plants described as Bog or Swamp Plants – nurserymen's catalogues have lists of them; yet none is suitable for a genuine bog. The Wild Purple Orchid, for example (*Cypripedium reginae*), with its rose coloured flowers, is listed as one. True it needs a damp situation – but it must be well drained. It wouldn't survive long in boggy ground.

A Bog-garden, however, is something quite different from a bog or bogland, where often peat is cut out and stacked up and dried for fuel – one sees this done in parts of Ireland: in Tipperary, for instance. Not many things of any garden value grow in a genuine bog. It is the habitat of mosses and grass-like rushes. (See page 49.)

Some plants like wetter situations than others but few will thrive where the moisture is permanently stagnant. And the ideal Bog-garden is the one where the amount of water can be controlled. It may be supplied from a tap or from a natural spring. A hose is necessary in the first instance, and a system of canals for irrigating the soil in the second.

The site chosen should naturally be the lowest part of the garden and preferably close to a pool or a steam. Sometimes soil is excavated to form a depression which is then given a foundation of puddled (water-tight) clay, which holds the moisture as effectually as a foundation of concrete. (See pages 88–89.) There are several ways of making a Bog-garden.

A MINIATURE BOG-GARDEN

A large pool can have a piece of ground projecting into it – a sort of peninsula which is made at the same time as the pool itself.

When excavating the soil for the pool, a piece of ground for the bog 'peninsula' is left isolated. This should be bricked round from the base upwards to strengthen the sides and prevent the soil from being washed away by the water in the pool.

The top course of bricks will be just below the surface, and an edging of stones or small rocks, placed on the bricks, will keep the specially prepared bog-soil, mostly peat or leafmould, from falling into the water. The stones must not be cemented together or the water will not be able to pass through them to reach the plants. They will eventually be hidden by suitable things like the Water-grass, *Juncus nodosus*, which likes gravelly wet soils.

The soil should be a peaty compost: sifted peat or leafmould, sand and loam or well-decayed vegetable matter, and it will replace the top 9 inches of soil removed from the 'peninsula.' It can be renewed from time to time but the roots of the plants should not be disturbed. Scoop away carefully any black, sour mud and add fresh coarse sand and more sifted leafmould.

Small flagstones, say, 9 inches square, sunk into the wet soil – on a firm foundation of stones and rubble – will be better than the usual rounded stepping-stones, though they won't be wanted at all in a very small Bog-garden. I suggest the depth of the water in the pool, surrounding the 'bog,' should not be more than 18 inches.

A LARGE BOG-GARDEN

Another type, with a cement, basin-like depression to hold the wet soil, can be planned on a much larger scale than the one just described.

Dig out soil to a depth of about 30 inches to form a basin and line it with cement. Before it dries, fix an overflow-pipe level with the surface to carry away any surplus water. (The method of lining the basin is the same as that for lining an ornamental pool. See pages 90–91.) The water is usually supplied to the Bog-garden by a tap in the garden, a pipe being attached to it and feeding the 'bog' periodically. The soil which will be put in the basin will of course be specially prepared and moisture-retentive. Without a supply of water in the garden, it will be necessary to use a longer pipe – a hose – attached to the kitchen-tap, though the rains will help and an occasional bucket of water is usually enough for a small area.

When the cement is dry, put in drainage material – rubble or broken bricks – to a depth of 6 inches and then fill up with a mixture of acid loam, coarse sand and sifted peat or leafmould. This compost suits most of the hardy Orchids admirably. You may require more coarse sand and perhaps a little lime-rubble for certain other Bog Plants. Before you reach the top, place a piece of perforated zinc against the entrance-hole of the over-flow-pipe to prevent it from being blocked by debris.

I prefer flagstones to stepping-stones dotted about a Bog-garden, for the simple reason that one must be able to walk about the area in comfort. Stepping-stones, with their rough, uneven tops, are more picturesque but tiring to the feet after a time.

With a tap in the garden, which means an easy supply of water, it is possible to have a Bog-garden to cover a good-sized area. And where there is a grassy slope, the water can be brought to the top by a pipe and then by means of a spray-line or some sort of spraying-apparatus, allowed to trickle down and make an oozy, wet site at the bottom. The apparatus is neces-sary to distribute the water over the full width of the slope.

The site should be near a pond or a stream and provided with a drainage-pipe or two. The slope can be kept as moist as you want it by means of the spray-line, but it will never be as wet and soggy as the ground at the bottom.

A damp grassy slope is an ideal place for naturalizing some of the miniature Narcissi: *Narcissus bulbocodium* and *N. cycla-mineus* are two tiny Daffodils that revel in such a position. (See also pages 48 and 49.)

By sinking pieces of rock to, say, a third of their depth into the grass to give the impression of a natural outcrop, one can have an attractive feature of rock-work and Bog-garden combined: a suggestion of a high Alpine-garden.

No attempt should be made to cover the slope with Alpine plants, but it should be left as a wild spot where one or two un-common things can be allowed to run wild. As well as the miniature Daffodils, there are several choice little Primulas like the deep rose-pink *Primula rosea* which would look beautiful on a damp, grassy slope. The grass should be clipped only when the foliage of any plants grown in it has died down completely.

Stone can be bought from many nurseries; there are several types, viz. Dorset Limestone, Mountain Limestone, Sussex Sandstone and Water-worn Limestone.

Set the plants near the stone: it doesn't matter whether in

front or behind. They will spread quickly if they are given the right soils. It would be triumph if you got the glorious blue *Gentiana verna* to flower. There are very few places in a garden where it will live – it likes the wet grassy slopes of the Swiss Alps but refuses to be transplanted.

When planting the Narcissi, remove a piece of turf, set the bulbs in position and replace the turf. Grow the Primulas in a deep rich moist loam close to the stone.

PLANTING THE BOG-GARDEN

As regards the choice of plants, gardeners usually divide these into four groups, viz. Shrubs, Bog Orchids; Carnivorous or Insectivorous plants; Herbaceous perennials. And many described in previous chapters (waterside plants, for example) may be used.

As most of these plants like shade, it may be necessary to grow a tree with wide-spreading branches, or a shrub that will throw shade during the sunniest part of the day. Ideally this would be a swamp-loving tree such as a Willow or an Alder or the Swamp Cypress (*Taxodium distichum*). For an artificial bog, however, such as I have described, something smaller than these would be required. The Caucasian Wing-nut (*Pterocarya fraxinifolia*) is a fine moisture-loving tree or, more often in this country, a bushy shrub, which thrives in well-drained moist soils. It is a native of the Caucasus and Persia and is found there in swampy places; it grows much taller and bigger than it does in Britain. It belongs to the Walnut family and has a corrugated bark, long leaves composed of many leaflets, and the female tree carries long attractive catkins in late summer. The Caucasian Wingnut can be kept small and shapely by judicious pruning and, with its wide-spreading head, affords plenty of shade. A fine tree for big swampy places.

But as most garden bogs are perforce artificial ones, and the roots of the trees cannot reach the water which is contained in a basin-like structure, we can choose almost any kind with a wide-spreading head. It should be planted a good distance away from the actual Bog, as the branches will spread out some distance.

The Indian Bean Tree (*Catalpa bignonioides*) ultimately reaches a height of about 50 feet and has a wide-spreading, much-branched head when planted away from other trees. The leaves are ovalish, the largest 10 inches long and 8 inches wide, and pale green in colour. The flowers, white with yellow markings, are carried in panicles in July and August.

There are numerous smallish trees to choose from – Magnolias; the Purple-leaved Beech (in its young state); the Scarlet Oak; Maples; and numberous Ornamental Prunuses (Cherries, Plums, Almonds).

Shrubs suitable for planting *in* the Bog-garden are few in number; and anyhow, unless the Bog is very large, we don't want more than one or two. (Miniature Bogs require none at all.)

The Bog Rosemary (*Andromeda polifolia*) is a tiny Heather-like shrub, seldom more than 12 inches high, and has small clusters of bright pink flowers in April and May. It is a failure in limy ground; it needs peaty, moist, acid places such as the made-up garden Bog.

The Bog Myrtle (*Myrica gale*) is not particularly ornamental but makes a good background plant for any of the flowers we might grow – perennials, Orchids, and Carnivorous plants. *Myrica gale* is a bushy shrub, from 2 to 4 feet tall; the flowers are carried in catkins during May and June; the leaves are small and a dark glossy green. The best place for it is on the edge of the Bog-garden. Like the *Andromeda*, it is a native of Britain.

The number and variety of plants to be grown will of course depend on the size of the Bog. If it is large and spacious, we can include some from all the four groups mentioned above. But for a miniature Bog-garden, which is all that most people can find room for nowadays, probably a few of the hardy Orchids will be chosen. Some of these are native plants. All are beautiful.

There are at least a dozen genera of hardy terrestrial Orchids (those that grow in soil as distinct from the epiphyte kinds which grow on trees). Not everybody agrees about the hardiness of all of them, however. And although they are popularly known as Bog plants, they need well-drained moist places, not the stagnant moisture of a swamp.

The rose-purple Orchid, *Arethusa bulbosa*, is listed as half hardy by most specialists; it is too tender for many districts in Britain and needs warm southern gardens, if it is to thrive and flower freely. Similarly, the lovely *Bletilla striata* is suitable only for our warmest gardens. And it really needs protection by a cloche during the winter when grown out of doors. (Hillier and Sons, of Winchester, describe it as 'A beautiful Chinese terrestrial Orchid. The large, rose or rose-purple flowers are borne in summer. Hardy in a sheltered, semi-shady site in peaty or leafy soil.') It isn't hardy enough for gardens around London, however.

Cypripedium and *Orchis* are the two genera which contain some of the hardiest and most suitable plants for our Bog-gardens. Those I have chosen here are lovely plants, exotic-looking, almost: something we like to show off to our friends.

It would be wisest to make certain that the Bog-patch is really suitable for them – that they will live and thrive there – before we order any, for they are expensive to buy.

Cypripedium calceolus is known colloquially as the 'Ladies' Slipper Orchid.' It is a good name, describing well the shape of the flower, the lower petal being developed into a large, inflated, slipper-like sac (labellum). The other species have the same type of flower, viz. a low pouch-like lip and prominent petals of a different colour. *C. calceolus* is a native plant, the rarest we have, and for that reason I put it first. It is indigenous only to England apparently and found now in woods on limestone in Yorkshire and Durham. The pouch-like lip is yellow and the petals chocolate-brown. This Orchid needs deep, moist, leafy soil in a cool shady place facing north. The edge of the Bog-garden is ideal for it. It flowers in May and June and grows about 12 inches tall. Like the other hardy species, the stems are erect, herbaceous, leafy and spring up again early in the year.

C. acaule (*humile*) is a North American species, blooming in May and June, about 9 inches tall. It carries a large, single flower, rosy-purple in colour with greenish sepals. It needs moist peaty soil with an admixture of grit and tiny stones. I've found that this species and all the hardy *Cypripedium* do best when grown in the shade of a smallish piece of rock. (See page 111.)

C. pubescens (*hirsutum*), from North America, has leafy stems usually about 18 inches tall; the flower consists of a yellow pouch lined with purple, and petals and sepals yellow-green and purple. This lovely rarity needs shade and shelter in most of our gardens and most, well-drained gritty soil.

C. reginae is the showiest of all the hardy species. The flowers are often carried in threes; the pouch is white flushed with rose;

the sepals or petals white. A magnificent flower which shows up beautifully against the light green leaves clothing the stem. This hardy North American Orchid is often grown in a shady part of a Rhododendron border. It flowers in June.

These 'Lady Slipper' Orchids are propagated by root-division in late spring. But they much resent root disturbance and may not survive it; where good specimens are growing and flowering well, I should certainly leave them alone. It is much wiser to buy the extra plants required from a nursery. *C. reginae* costs about 10s. 6d. a root.

In nature they are often found in damp woodlands or at the edge of cool boglands; sometimes on sandy plains and moist grasslands. No attempt should be made to shift these lovely wildings and transplant them to a garden. The result is invariably a failure.

This is partly explained by the dependence of Orchids on a fungal growth in the soil for their health and well-being; similarly the fungus depends on the Orchids – it is a kind of symbiotic relationship: both plants and fungus contribute something to the well-being of the other. If the plants *have* to be shifted, remove a wide, deep piece of soil with them.

The miniature Bog-garden, described on page 118, is an excellent place for one or two of these rare, lovely plants. It can be a sort of show place for them.

Orchis is a large genus of terrestrial Orchids, perennial plants, with erect leafy stems which die down in the winter. The flowers, usually small and some very attractive, come in a spike on the upper part of the stems.

There are several British species; and these plants do better in our gardens than the exotic ones; yet some of the latter thrive wonderfully when given the right situations and the right soil. For instance, you can see some fine specimens of *Orchis elata* from Algeria, and *O. maderensis* from Madeira in the Savill Gardens. They are grown in peat beds (which retain moisture all through the summer) and in shady places.

The Bog-garden is the ideal place for *Orchis*. And like the *Cypripedium* they flourish luxuriantly when planted against rocks embedded in the soil.

The tubers should be planted from August to late October and set 2 inches below the surface – in most gardens they are grown in equal parts of fibrous peat or sifted leafmould and coarse sand. The important thing is never to let this compost dry out during the summer months. Newly planted specimens are often watered regularly during the flowering season and given weak doses of liquid manure about every ten days – it should be applied only if the soil is quite moist. (In the Bog-garden it always is.) As long ago as 1725, Bradley, in his *Family Dictionary*, said: 'In the culture of the *Orchis*, the gardener must give it a moist earth and a northern exposition.' (Aspect.) The tubers of some of them may be bought from most bulb specialists and should not be disturbed once they are established.

The chief species which grow wild in Britain are *O. incarnata*; *O. latifolia*; *O. maculata*; *O. mascula*; *O. militaris*; *O. morio*; *O. purpurea.*

Orchis latifolia is the Marsh Orchid and succeeds in peaty, moist soil in partial shade at the Savill Gardens, where it grows along with other species and some of the hardy *Cypripedium* described above. The flowers, set close together on a spike, are red or purple, the leaves lance-shaped, glaucous-green and often marked with brownish streaks. A good healthy specimen will reach a height of 18 inches or more. (Native of Europe, including Britain, Asia.)

O. incarnata (Early Marsh Orchis) closely resembles the above species but blooms earlier. The flowers are variable in colour – usually shades of flesh-pink to red. The leaves are narrower than in *O. latifolia*. The plant grows about 12 inches high.

O. maculata (the Spotted Orchis). It has deep purplish-brown blotches on its leaves and pale purple flowers carried in a compact spike. These are at their best in June and a magnificent sight in the Bog-garden if you can have them massed somewhere in partial shade. I have seen this Orchid grown on the banks of a stream, with the dwarf Rush, *Scirpus cernuus*, with drooping grass-like leaves (almost like a mop) grown as an edging by the waterside. The Rush was set out in pots and lifted in the autumn and housed for the winter, as it is on the tender side. (See chapter 13 for a description of the species.)

O. mascula is the Early Purple Orchis, which blooms in spring; it is the most common of our native species. It has deep green oblong leaves marked with purple spots and erect spikes of purple flowers carried on stems reaching a height of from 9 to 18 inches. This species grows tall in shady places where the soil is deep and moist. A native of Europe (including Britain), North Africa and Western Siberia.

O. militaris (known as the Military Orchis) is a very rare species. The flowers are carried freely in dense, oblong spikes and are a lovely shade of purple. The stems are from 1 to 2 feet long and the leaves broadly oval to oblong. It is a native of Europe and sometimes found wild in the south of England.

O. morio blooms in early summer and is known to collectors as the green-winged Orchis: it has green veins on the petals. The flowers come in loose spikes on stems 6 to 8 inches long, and are usually pinkish-purple in colour. It is a native of Europe (including Britain) and Western Asia.

O. purpurea has flowers variable in colour, usually rose, spotted with purple, and oblong-shaped leaves, 3 to 5 inches long. The species blooms in May. Native of Europe and found in moist woods in Britain.

The most striking of all the Orchis we grow out of doors is the Madeira Orchis, *Orchis maderensis* (syn. *foliosa*). It is so beautiful in fact that many gardeners prefer to grow it in pots in a cold shady greenhouse. But in a well-drained bed of fibrous peat and coarse sand in the Bog-garden it will thrive and flower profusely during May, provided the situation is fairly shady. The plant reaches a height of 18 inches or so (2 feet under glass) and carries compact spikes of lovely rose-purple flowers. It needs a deep, rich peaty soil which is constantly damp all through the summer.

If grown in a pot, give it a compost of equal parts of fibrous peat or leafmould, rich garden loam (sifted) and silver sand. Make the compost firm; use a 6-inch pot and plant the tubers, about three to a pot, 1 inch below the surface. Water copiously as soon as growth commences and till the foliage fades; then keep reasonably dry through the dormant period. Give a little weak liquid manure every 10 days, when the flower-buds begin to form. The plants are carefully repotted every third year.

O. elata is allied to the above species – a taller plant though, with stems over 2 feet high and large, violet-purple flowers in spikes 8 inches or more long. They stand out well above the attractive green leaves. The plant is a native of Algeria.

O. laxiflora, the Guernsey Orchis or the Loose Orchis, is found wild in Guernsey and Jersey but not in Britain. Its stems are from 1 to 3 feet high and have loose spikes of deep red-purple flowers, which bloom in early summer; the leaves are lanceolate (tapering to both ends), 3 to 6 inches long. This Orchis needs deep moist peaty loam and partial shade. It is a native of Europe; in Jersey and Guernsey; it is usually found in wet meadows.

Orchis and *Cypripedium* are the two chief families of hardy Orchids and they contain some of the loveliest of all the garden kinds. In a small Bog-garden, such as the 'peninsula' type described on page 118, one species grouped separately produces the most striking effect – perhaps *Cypripedium reginae* or *Orchis maderensis*, and as a foil to the flowers nothing could be better than the delicate, lacy foliage of the Hardy Maidenhair Fern, *Adiantum pedatum* (see page 111).

There are other families of hardy Orchids, such as *Epipactia*; *Goodyera*; *Habenaria*; *Listeria*; but these are less often seen in our gardens and many are difficult to get.

Tubers of some of the hardy *Orchis* and *Cypripedium* can be obtained from Hillier and Sons, Winchester; and W. E. Ingwersen, Ltd., East Grinstead; and Sphagnum moss peat from the Irish Peat Moss Company, Bristol, 1.

CARNIVOROUS PLANTS

Carnivorous Plants (Insectivorous Plants) are those which have the ability to catch insects and the power of consuming them. The insect or animal tissue supplies nitrogen in an assimilable form. (Many of these plants grow in boggy places, and those described here are all suitable for the Bog-garden.) There are Carnivorous plants which have leaves with sensitive, glandular hairs discharging a sticky fluid which captures and digests insects and other tiny creatures. The nutrition in the form of nitrogen is absorbed by the leaves and feeds the plants. Others capture insects by bladders or pitchers; for instance, the *Nepenthes*, Pitcher Plants, natives of the steamy bogs of Indo-Malaya and Madagascar. The pitchers are developed at the tip of the tendrils or the leaves and are roughly speaking bag-shaped and have a small hood over the opening at the top. Flies, insects and the like enter the pitchers and are drowned in the fluid contained at the bottom. The decomposed matter is then absorbed by the pitcher and helps to nourish the plant.

Aldrovanda versiculosa is a rootless, floating plant with leaves which grow in whorls, and measure about an inch across. The flowers are white and raised above the water. It blooms in July. The leaves, provided with bristles in the centre, close and entrap any insects when they alight on them. The plant needs shade and should be grown in the shallow water of a pool or a stream.

Darlingtonia californica is the Californian Pitcher Plant, one of the carnivore with tall tubular or funnel-shaped leaves, 1 to 2 feet tall, hooded at the top and forming pitchers, through which insects enter. These modified leaves are green below with the upper part mottled white. The flowers are yellowish-green with dark reddish-brown veins; but quite inconspicuous and eclipsed by the curiously-shaped leaves. The plant is hardy in most places and needs a boggy, shady spot. A compost of peat and chopped Sphagnum (Bog-moss) with plenty of sharp sand and some broken up charcoal is an ideal medium. Its habitat is the mountain swamps of California. It does well in a Bog-garden, set among hardy Ferns.

Propagation is by side shoots which are taken in summer, set in small pots and kept under a cloche till established. Or the plants can be raised from seed sown on damp peaty soil; the seed-pots must be stood in saucers of water till the seeds have germinated.

Dionaea muscipula (Venus's Fly-trap). It traps flies by its curiously constructed leaves, which close when one of the three bristles in the centre is lightly touched twice,* the flies being then entrapped and and subsequently digested. The flowers are white and come in flattish clusters about an inch across in June and July. *Dionaea muscipula* is a native of North and South Carolina, its natural habitat being damp, mossy places near bogs – the haunt of insects, on which the plant lives. This carnivore needs a warm, sheltered spot in a Bog-garden. Many gardeners, however, prefer to grow it in a pot in a cold greenhouse.

Drosera. (The word is from the Greek *droseros*, dewy; the gland-tipped hairs on the leaves are dewy.) The plants are known as the Sundews; some species are greenhouse plants; other hardy perennials suitable for sunny places in the Bog-garden and flourishing in a well-drained mixture of Sphagnum moss and fibrous peat or leafmould.

* One of the three bristles must be lightly touched *twice*, or the leaf must be more heavily knocked before it closes and traps the insect.

24

Iris sibirica.

25

An informal pool flanked by large stepping stones leading to a Summer House.

There are several native species. *D. anglica* has narrow leaves, the blade (the flattened part of the leaf) is about an inch long; the flowers rose-white come in a cluster. A native of Europe, including Britain; but more common in Scotland and Ireland than in England.

D. longifolia has erect leaves, gradually tapering into the root-stalk; the flowers are white. Habitat: Europe and bogs in some parts of Britain.

D. rotundifolia is our most common species and has rosettes of roundish leaves ¾ inch to 2 inches long; and slender stems 4 inches high, carrying white flowers in summer, rise from the centre of the leaf-rosettes.

The leaves of the *Drosera* grow close to the soil, and insects alighting on them cause the sensitive, viscid hairs to curve inwards and entrap them. The leaves close and then open again after the insect tissues have been absorbed and digested.

Drosophyllum lusitanicum belongs to the Droseraceae Family and is mostly grown as a curiosity in a pot in a cool greenhouse, where it must have a minimum temperature of 45°F. through the winter months. I have seen it out of doors, however, in a Bog-garden, where it was grown as a show-plant – it was taken indoors again in October and housed till the following May.

This carnivore makes a pleasing sub-shrubby plant, 12 inches tall, with a woody stem carrying a small flattish spike of yellow flowers in May. The leaves are long and narrow (4 to 8 inches in length and ⅛ inch wide) and bear sticky glands. Insects alight on the substance and adhere to it, and when their bodies have decomposed they are absorbed by the leaves. Like many carnivorous plants, *D. lusitanicum* is more curious than beautiful.

The specific epithet, *lusitanicum*, means 'of Portugal'; the plant is a native of that country and of Morocco. In Portugal it is sometimes suspended in its pot from the ceiling of a house and actually used as a fly-catcher.

Sarracenia contains several species with attractive flowers, indeed, *S. flava* is a beautiful garden plant and so is *S. purpurea*, and both are hardy enough for most gardens in this country.

The hardy species are fine plants for boggy places. A good compost for them consists of equal parts of peat and Sphagnum moss.

The pitcher-like leaves vary considerably in height: some are as little as 2 inches tall, some are 2 feet; there is also great

E

diversity of shapes, some being cup-shaped, others cylindrical or trumpet-like. And the colouring is remarkable, varying from green and yellow to red, crimson and deep purple; and most of the pitchers are streaked with contrasting colours.

As in all these pitcher-plants, the purpose of the pitchers is to ensnare and catch insects. They are attracted by the honey-like substance secreted by the glands on the lids and are prevented from escaping by downward-pointing hairs which lead to a slippery area. When they reach this, they fall into the liquid at the bottom of the pitcher and are drowned.

The pitchers are stemless and spring up directly from the rhizomes beneath the soil; and the flowers come on slender, leafless stalks, which rise from the crowns of the plants. They vary from 1 to 3 inches across and are usually a shade of yellow, red, crimson and purple.

S. drummondi has pitchers about 20 inches tall, attractively variegated – green and purple mottled with white; the flowers are greenish-purple. A lovely plant and a native of North America.

S. flava has erect narrow pitchers 2 feet or more tall, of a greenish-yellow colour, and veined with purple. The flowers are yellow and some of the most striking of all the species.

S. purpurea is completely hardy and usually singled out for cultivation in the Bog-garden; it is not difficult to grow, given the right conditions. The pitchers are about 8 inches tall, green in colour and veined red, the flowers greenish-purple.

Plant this species in a damp, sunny spot and it will live for years and flower freely every spring. It may be propagated by seed or by division in March or April.

All the species of *Sarracenia* may be increased by seed; and the varieties by division. But the new plants will not flower till they are several years old.

Utricularia are the Bladderworts; the plants catch in their small spherical bladders minute animals, such as larvae of flies, mosquitos and the like; and the decomposed animals provide nitrogenous food for the plants. Some of the species are aquatics, living in water, floating or submersed; others from the tropical regions are terrestrial.

The best-known species in Britain is our native *U. vulgaris*, a hardy aquatic which grows in ponds or tubs in 2 feet of water. (It is known as the Common Bladderwort.) The stems are often

18 inches long and have several branches with finely dissected leaves bearing numerous traps (bladders). The plant has clusters of bright yellow flowers on stems 4 to 8 inches long which are raised several inches out of the water. It requires no soil.

U. intermedia (another native) is less commonly seen and has delicate-looking fern-like foliage and bladders borne on leafless branches. The flowers are pale yellow and not so conspicuous as those of *U. vulgaris*.

Both species are completely hardy and pass the winter hibernating in a bud-state at the bottom of the water; both are excellent plants for the aquarium.

HERBACEOUS PERENNIALS FOR THE BOG-GARDEN

A great number of the perennials we grow in our herbaceous borders would do well in the Bog-garden: Foxgloves, for instance, which like moist shady places, and the Welsh Poppy (*Meconopsis cambrica*); but it would be unwise to grow either, since they seed themselves so freely. And in a Bog-garden, where growing conditions are ideal for these plants, we'd never get rid of them and they would soon over-run everything else. The best place for them is the woodland. Lupins like deep moist soil, so do Delphiniums; but they would look out of place in a bog (they are essentially border-plants) and, moreover, they require reasonably dry conditions through the winter months.

Herbaceous perennials that will thrive in Bog-gardens usually need shade and are often recommended for planting in woodlands. Several species of Anemone are suitable for growing among trees and one, namely, *Anemone rivularis*, should be planted in damp peat and according to a specialist 'is ideal for setting by the side of a pool or a stream.' I have seen it in Bog-gardens in the south of England, but it will flourish in most parts of the country. It grows 18 inches tall and has clusters of white flowers with blue anthers. The plant blooms in May and rather resembles *A. narcissiflora* (with yellow anthers) which blooms later. Plant the bog species in damp peat, to which is added coarse sand and some lime-rubble or granite chips. *A. rivularis* is a native of northern India and Ceylon.

Coreopsis are well known and special favourites with gardeners for a late summer display in sunny flower-borders. They belong to the Daisy family and are chiefly yellow or orange in colour.

But *C. rosea* thrives and flowers profusely in sunny swampy places. Its flowers are rose-pink and about an inch across and come on slender branching stems 12 to 18 inches high; the leaves are narrow-linear (grass-like). A native of the eastern United States.

Filipendula are mostly grown in, and recommended for, the herbaceous border; they need a deep rich loam and partial shade. But two species at least prefer the moister conditions of the Bog-garden; these are *F. camtschatica* and *F. purpurea*. The first is a tall plant and best grown on the edge of a 'bog'; in wet soils (well-drained) it may reach 6 feet or more in height; it has dark green, lobed leaves and large clusters of fragrant rose-pink flowers.

F. purpurea is a charming 'bog' perennial with flattish clusters of crimson flowers and attractive dark green, divided leaves. Height: 2 to 3 feet.

Geum rivale is the Water Avens, a herbaceous perennial often seen in the front row of a border and not – usually – in a very flourishing state. Plant it in the Bog-garden, and it looks quite different – more healthy and robust. It grows 12 inches tall and has rose-salmon coloured flowers in June and July and dark green, strawberry-like leaves. LEONARD'S VARIETY is the best form.

The Day Lilies (*Hemerocallis*) do best in semi-shady places; and one of the most beautiful for the garden 'bog' is *Hemerocallis flava* with delightfully scented, Lily-like, lemon-yellow flowers. It is 2 feet tall and blooms from July to September. Its rush-like foliage suggests the waterside.

Hosta are grown primarily for their large cool-looking leaves. They, too, suggest the water and the waterside. (The flowers are not liked very much – in fact some gardeners cut them off when they are in bud.) Various species are described in chapter 13.

Inula helenium is a native plant with large, bright yellow Daisy-like flowers carried singly on stems 4 or 5 feet high. The leaves are big, coarse-looking and an excellent foil to the flowers. The plant flourishes most luxuriantly in deep, moist loams.

Kirengeshoma palmata is a Japanese plant and something of a rarity in our gardens. It needs a moist shady position, which is often difficult to find in the average herbaceous border. It grows 2 feet tall, has large, papery, lobed leaves (hairy on both sides), and clusters of yellow, bell-shaped flowers at the end of the stems. They are at their best in autumn. (*Kirengeshoma* is a Japanese word, meaning yellow-flowered.)

There is a hardy Lily called the Swamp Lily, which likes deep, moist soils, but can only be grown in the Bog-garden if the soil is impeccably drained. (The bulbs are apt to rot in winter if the moisture becomes stagnant and turns sour.) If you plant this species, with its lovely bright orange-red flowers, put plenty of coarse sand round the bulbs – many gardeners lift them in the autumn and store them for the winter. The name of the plant is *Lilium superbum*. It is inclined to grow very tall in shade and may reach 8 feet.

Other species I have come across in Bog-gardens are the Canadian Lily, *Lilium canadense*, with bright orange-yellow re-curved flowers; and *L. pardalinum*, orange-scarlet, known as the Panther Lily. Both are best on the edge of a 'bog'.

Lobelia cardinalis has been called the deepest scarlet flower in cultivation. It is so beautiful that it is worth planting it out in its pot; it seldom survives our winters, unless it is grown in warm, southern gardens. And it may not live there in 'bogs' if the soil lacks sufficient drainage material. The hybrid forms are thought to be hardier. Var. QUEEN VICTORIA, with crimson foliage and rich scarlet flowers, is recommended by gardeners.

Lychnis (the Campions) are mentioned in chapter 1, page 31. *L. chalcedonica* is the favourite one for shady, moist places. (See chapter 2, page 50.)

Lythrum (Purple Loose-strife; Willow-weed). See chapter 2, page 50.

Primulas. (See chapter 1, pages 23–26.)

Senecio clivorum (often described under the specific name *Ligularia clivorum*). This is the most ornamental of the herbaceous Senecios and does best where its roots can get down to plenty of water; hence its frequent use by the side of pools and streams. It is equally at home in the Bog-garden, where the soil is peaty and moist. It has large, roundish leaves and a brilliant orange, candelabra-shaped inflorescence; the stems are 3 feet high. A most useful 'bog' plant, since it blooms in late summer and early autumn.

Trillium grandiflorum is one of the American Wood Lilies and a popular plant for growing in a moist woodland – it will be found in many parts of the Savill Gardens and grows there in wet peaty soil. The plant has pure white flowers (2 inches across) on stems about a foot tall which stand up conspicuously above the cool-looking foliage. It blooms in April and May, the flowers often turning pale pink as they age.

Our last plant is the rarest and one seldom seen outside the warmest, southern gardens in these islands. It is the lovely, exotic-looking Arum Lily, with its dark green polished leaves and white spathes, which are much valued for indoor decoration. It is sometimes grown in a pool, the rhizomes being set well below the ice-level in case of severe frost. (They should be about 30 inches under water.) In the Isle of Wight it is hardy enough to grow in a flower border or in the Bog-garden, provided it is given good sharp drainage in the soil which must be rich and loamy and constantly moist. More often than not it is sunk in its pot in the ground and lifted in the autumn. The plant is then housed till the following June. The specific name of the plant is *Zantedeschia aethiopica*. The bulbs we get from northern Transvaal are reasonably hardy (the winters there are often severe); and the plants stand up well to frosts in our country.

CHAPTER TEN

Fountains and Cascades

GARDEN FOUNTAINS are entirely ornamental features. We don't drink from them, for instance, unless we happen to be very thirsty, and even then it would be unwise to do so, since the water is used over and over again and is consequently scarcely fit for human consumption. On the other hand, there are some which are supplied by water coming from the main, which is always fresh. It is conducted to the jet or spout either by a pipe attached to a tap in the garden (an ordinary hose is used), or by a pipe laid underground and connected to a natural source, perhaps a spring or a running stream. But most garden fountains nowadays are supplied by water pumped up out of a stone basin or pool by a small electric motor installed in or near the pool. The same water is used till it is renewed by the owner.

In ancient Greek and Roman times many of the fountains erected in towns and cities were utilitarian, ample draw-basins supplying the people with the water they needed. And many were ornately sculptured in stone or marble and were objects of great beauty in the city squares and gardens. Our own drinking-fountains – the first was erected in London, by the way, in 1859 – are very modest-looking things compared with them. Similarly, our garden fountains have become much more simple in design. There is no room in the modern garden for spectacular water features such as those we can see in the grounds of some of our big country houses planned in the nineteenth century or earlier. At Chatsworth, Derbyshire, for example, there is a fountain that throws a jet of water 260 feet in the air; and there are cascades, waterfalls and other amazingly intricate waterworks. These things needed an enormous staff of gardeners for their maintenance and care. Today they are delightful to see, but nobody wants to possess them.

We can't of course have a fountain in a pool where we grow hardy Water-lilies, since these plants need still water which doesn't vary in temperature. (See illustration.) The double-pool design (see page 60), which provides for two pools of equal size connected by a false canal, solves the problem effectually. (One end of the canal is closed or bricked up to prevent any flow of water from the fountain into the Lily Pool.) The design can be varied in many ways, depending on the ingenuity of the gardener. The fountain can be put in the canal and allowed to play at an angle, the water spraying in the opposite direction to the Lilies. Or there can be two jets in the canal, both spouting their water at an angle into the pool.

The Drip-fountain, where the water runs from an object on a wall – often a carved mask – is probably the only kind which causes the minimum disturbance to the water in the basin below. (See Fig. 13, page 143.) If the basin or pool is large enough some of the smaller Nymphaea can be grown in it. The usual shape for such a pool is almost always semi-circular; its width from the wall to the rim (half the width of the diameter if the pool were circular) should not be less than 6 feet. It would be safe to plant the Lilies in a container sunk about a couple of feet from the rim. The plants will be undisturbed there.

The smallest type of fountain, which is much in demand these days, has a correspondingly small basin. The tub-sized kind, with a diameter of, say, 18 inches or less, usually has a gurgling jet roughly 9 inches or so high, which it is always cool and refreshing to see and hear.

The more powerful jet which throws up water to perhaps 10 or 12 feet cannot be used in very small pools. For one thing, the falling water would splash over the sides of the basin and be-spatter the surrounding ground or paving; for another thing, it would look out of place; usually the basin or pool is a little larger in width or in diameter than the height of the fountain jet.

The height of course depends on the pressure of the water; and for one of these exiguous pool-basins an electric pump seems wasted.

An ordinary plastic pipe attached to a tap is all that is re-quired. The pipe can be easily hidden or disguised and can be sunk in the ground contained in a larger drainage pipe or conduit and covered over with soil. The pipe, with a nozzle attached, then carries on down the inside of the concrete pool, and is held firmly against the side by a sort of metal staple (fixed in position when the cement is wet). Use a large, up-turned flower-pot to keep the end of the hose with the nozzle upright in the water. The drainage hole in the pot is about ¾ inch across and usually big enough to take the hose. (The hole can be made larger, if necessary, by chipping off a piece of the earthenware.) Chip out a piece also from the side so that the pot stands firm when it covers the vertical piece of hose. Let the nozzle come just above the surface of the water. (It is possible now to buy what is known as an ornament-base or support to hold the hose in position at the bottom of the pool, and also a glass-fibre jet support which stands on top of it. See information below.)

The fountain is then ready to play; and you vary the pressure of the water and the consequent height of the jet by a turn of the tap. It can vary from a mere gurgle to a graceful jet rising several feet in height. And you can drink from it if you wish! An overflow pipe is usually fixed level with the top of the pool.

Another natural source is rain water supplied from the guttering of a house and stored in a large tank. Metal piping ⅜ inch in diameter, such as can be obtained from an electrician's, is used. It is attached to the bottom of the tank and brought down under the soil and the stone paving or gravel surrounding the pool. It is easily bent and shaped to go down the inside of the pool and stand erect in the water. The supply of water is not permanent – unless the weather is continuously wet – and nor-mally this sort of fountain spray has a limited existence.

The modern method is by far the easiest and the best. We use what is popularly known as a Fountain Kit. It has a sub-mersible pump which is stood in the water on a ledge or shelf built at the edge of the pool, and is the best type of pump for pools more than 4 feet wide, since it has the fountain-adjuster attached to it and is therefore easy to reach – one doesn't have to stretch out across the water to the middle of the pool. The pump has a length of plastic tubing which is sunk to the bottom of the water and emerges out through an ornament-base made of stone or lead, with several access holes – it is a more efficient base than the inverted flower-pot described above. The tubing is held in place above it by a glass-fibre jet support, the jet itself coming just above the water level. An inlet strainer is attached to the pump and prevents tiny particles entering and blocking the fine holes in the fountain jet. A weatherproof cable connec-

E*

tor is supplied with about 10 feet of sealed cable, the latter being connected to the pump under the water. Extra length of ordinary cable is required to reach back to the mains and costs about 6d. a foot.

Normally the height of the fountain jet is 5 feet or so; the jets themselves are varied in design and produce many delightful types of spray. (See Fig. 13, page 143.) By turning the adjuster, the height can be raised or lowered, the tall sprays being more suitable for large formal pools.

Fountains, like statues, are said to be out of place in the wild garden; those with elaborate fan-shaped sprays would be of course, but it is possible to have a low gurgling jet near the main pool, rising from its own supply of water. The sound has a relaxing effect and one often likes to sit near a pool during the hot sunny weather.

The jet can reach the edge of the main pool, if the nozzle is suitably adjusted, and the water can spout up out of a bed of pebbles. I have seen this done in quite small Water-gardens. The electric pump was placed in a small pool – a tub-like depression, concreted, and about 2 feet across – and connected with another depression concreted and containing the pebbles, the water flowing back into the supply pool. A delightful and quite natural effect for a wild garden. The supply pool was covered with a stone slab, and the cable leading to the mains in the house was hidden in the undergrowth; it was removed at the end of the autumn and stored indoors for the winter.

In the formal garden the cable is best sunk in earthen pipes under the paving, and the length leading to the house should be camouflaged as efficiently as possible. Usually a formal pool and fountain are not far from the house, and it is not a difficult matter to conceal electric cabling and other attachments. The cost of a Fountain Kit such as the one I have described is round about £10.

As it is not possible to grow anything in a fountain-pool, arrangements are often made to grow a few plants somewhere in the background. The most striking effect is obtained of course when the surround is simply stone paving and a well-mown lawn.

Suitable plants are those which are adapted to cultivation in tubs, or stone vases. These receptacles are in keeping with the formal lay-out. Low-growing flowers and shrubs can both be used. Plant them in pots which fit nicely into these ornamental containers. The plants in their pots can then be removed very easily when they have finished flowering and replaced with other suitable things which follow.

Begin in April with dwarf Tulips of the same colour: one good-sized pot is enough. When the flowers begin to fade, take out the pot and replace them with something else. In May one of the gorgeous Japanese Azaleas – a Kurume perhaps. It should last the month. It won't matter if it doesn't, because there is now an abundance of things to choose from – anything grown in a hot-house can come outside and be stood in its pot in the container. Arum Lilies, white or yellow. Any of the vivid coloured Cinerarias. Scarlet Geraniums. These will last till late autumn. My own choice would be one of the dwarf Japanese Maples (*Acer*), with finely-dissected, fern-like leaves, and either a lovely shade of soft green which turns scarlet in autumn, or a bronzy crimson colour which turns a richer deeper crimson later.

Where the pool and its stone surround are sunk below the surface of the garden and enclosed, or partially enclosed, by a low retaining wall – a favourite arrangement for a formal pool – trailing Alpines, like Aubrietia and Arabis, may be grown in the crevices of the stone wall, or set in a narrow border at the top. Or Ferns like the Hart's Tongue (page 113) which are less showy may be used.

The rock Campanulas are ideal for growing in crevices, and *Campanula portenschlagiana*, with light bluish bells (on stems 6 inches long) is one of the most suitable. Moreover, it blooms practically all the summer.

And in the paving surround itself a single, tall flower can be planted in a space specially made for it. (When setting the slabs in position, leave a square of about 9 inches of soil uncovered. Take out the existing soil and replace it with good deep leafy loam.) Nothing could be better for such a place than the tall 5-foot Chimney Campanula, *C. pyramidalis*, with slender stems covered with bright, blue, saucer-shaped flowers. It can be very easily raised from seed (treated as a biennial) or bought from any nursery for about 3s. It is often used for indoor decoration and grown for this purpose in a pot. When planted in the paving stone surround, it should be set immediately opposite the fountain in the pool.

WATERFALLS AND CASCADES

How high is a waterfall. I suppose it shouldn't be less than 6 feet. Half that and it would be called a cascade. And possibly the only kind of waterfall we can have in a garden is the cascade type, consisting of a series of falls a few feet high. The grand, spectacular example is at Chatsworth, where many cascades descend in a sort of water-staircase cut out of a grass slope.

A waterfall would require a 6-foot declivity, then, and a lot of excavating done, apart from the motive power required to force the water up that distance. Cliff-like declivities occur occasionally in the grounds of vast estates. There is one at Waddesdon Manor, a quarry-like feature which serves as a background to a rock-garden.*

In the small modern garden the usual type of cascade is that flowing into a pool, from which the water is pumped up again to the top of the slope, the action going on continuously as in the case of the fountain-pool.

The cascade basins or pools can be made of cement, with a wide lip in front to enable the water to flow over easily, or of fibre-glass (bought from a nursery). Two are sufficient for the average-sized garden and they are stood in suitable depressions on a slope, which extends upwards no further and no higher than the length of the plastic hose (about 10 feet), through which the water is pumped. The pump, similar to the fountain-pump, is stood on a ledge in the bottom (supply) pool; the plastic hose or tubing comes from it and is hidden in the soil on its way up to the top cascade. There it emerges out of the soil (or from its camouflage) and supplies the water which then comes tumbling down to the bottom pool again. As with the Fountain-pool, described above, the same water is used over and over again. (See Fig. 11.)

The supply pool should have a surface area of about 30 square feet. Most of the pools built for this type of cascade are roughly 5 feet square, or are circular with a diameter of about 6 feet.

Since there is a constant flow of water into the supply pool and consequently some surface disturbance there and a slight change of temperature, it is not advisable to grow any of the

* There is no Water-garden at Waddesdon, but there are two magnificent fountains. The most famous is the one on the South Front, with white marble sculptured figures in the Italian Renaissance style.

Water-lilies that require a largish area in which to expand. However, I have seen the reasonably small variety ODORATA SULPHUREA with fragrant yellow flowers growing well in one of these pools. (See page 67 for a description of the plant.) It was grown in a plastic container put on a ledge made at the edge of the pool (a concrete one), where there wasn't a great deal of surface movement. The chief danger, of course, comes from the moving water down the slope, which cools the bottom pool.

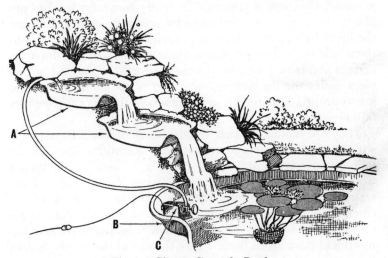

Fig. 11. Shows Cascade Pools

A = Cascade Pools   B = Supply Pool   C = Electric Motor

There are however plenty of tough, hardy things that can be grown in it. They are best planted in a container. The dwarf Reed Maces (*Typha*) are an excellent choice and may be planted near the centre of the pool. They need a loamy soil and shallow water. (See page 109.) The smallest, *Typha minima*, is about 12 inches tall. (The tallest plants, by the way, should come at the bottom of the slope – around or *in* the pool.) Another fine plant is the Water Mint, *Mentha aquatica*, a native species which delights in shallow water. It has oval leaves and clusters of very fragrant lilac-coloured flowers. In water it will often reach a height of 4 feet. It is best grown on a shelf close to the edge of the pool and is very hardy.

Menyanthes trifoliata is yet another native, a true hardy aquatic which will grow practically anywhere near water – or in it. It often creeps from the bank into the water and may be grown in a container on a ledge like the other two. It has olive-green leaves, composed of 3 leaflets. The flowers are white with red stamens, the petals fringed; they are small, bell-shaped and come in clusters. The plant is inclined to spread very rapidly and must be divided up every so often.

Some sort of camouflage may be required to hide the edges of the two cascade-pools; this is necessary when fibre-glass pools are used. Concrete is preferred by many gardeners, as they are able to fix in position (with cement) stones or small rocks near the lip to help spread the water as widely as possible – without them, it is apt to gush down in a single narrow stream. Moreover certain plants may be grown near the rocks, or planted in crevices under the lip. Several small Ferns like moist places and are appropriate plants for growing where they are splashed by falling water.

They are modest-looking things, being simply foliage plants with no showy flowers to attract one's attention. After all, the falling water is the important thing in a cascade. My choice would be the common Hart's Tongue Fern, which loves water and can be grown with its roots in a crevice of the cascade. A smaller variety is *Phyllitis scolopendrium* Var. RAMO-CHRISTATUM, which is not more than 6 inches high and has rosettes of dark green fronds. Like the rest of the family, it does best in partial shade, and is evergreen.

Another water-loving Fern is the North American Sensitive Fern (*Onoclea sensibilis*), a deciduous plant with deeply-divided fronds, 2 to 3 feet tall. It should be planted close to the edge of the cascade and will flourish wonderfully in loamy soil on a ledge in the water.

The sides of the cascades are often edged with rock. It must be a good quality rock, and where strata are visible, the lines or layers must all run the same way when the rocks are set in position. Place the largest at the bottom; above them smaller ones and the smallest at the top.

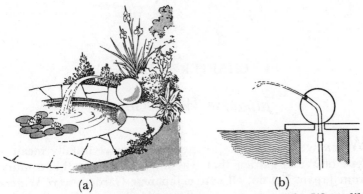

(a)   (b)

Fig. 12. (a) Small pool designed with fountain for tender Water-lily growing in a container. (b) Shows pipe-line under paving, and method of leading pipe through concrete ball.

Fig. 13. Shows an attractive 3-tier fountain-spray.

CHAPTER ELEVEN

Japanese Water-Gardens

WHEN WE mention a Japanese Garden we usually mean a type of Water-garden that was introduced into this country from Japan. Yet not all native Japanese Gardens were Water-gardens. There were many different kinds of gardens, but usually water in some form or other – a pool, a stream, a fountain – was the chief feature of the lay-out. Or a feature such as an expanse of raked sand and a few rocks were used to suggest it. (See page 15.) Garden design was often influenced by oriental philosophic thought. There was a feeling of serenity and repose in the lay-out and the arrangement of the plants and ornaments chosen. A great deal was in miniature; much of it was symbolic. A Japanese landscape gardener once said: 'My lake is the world. The fountain playing in its basin is me and my possessions. The sea I glimpse beyond the lake is the universe, from which everything comes and to which everything returns.'

We don't think so deeply about garden design in this country. And the Japanese garden is often planned as a feature of the garden proper. In one respect it does resemble the oriental pattern, viz. it is planned in miniature. Everything is small – pools, bridges, fountains, and plants. There are miniature 'mountains' (made from the soil excavated from the pool); a miniature 'island' (in Japan the 'island' frequently represented a tortoise or a crane, symbols of long life); a tiny bridge, arched and built of stone or wood; and there are hollows which represent valleys.

The lay-out is in fact a landscape in miniature. In our modern gardens, where space is restricted, it would be wise to concentrate on one or two of these features, say, a pool with a bridge and one or two rocks placed at the edge of the pool. Perhaps a summer-house, facing them, and, if possible, at the top of a slope. It should of course be oriental in design and big enough to seat several people.

26 A Formal pool enclosed by a low wall, Clare College Cambridge.

—*Photo H. Smith*

27
A very neat
informal pond.

—*Photo L. Perkins*

28

Informal pool with edging
of Ornamental Grasses.

29

Glyceria aquatica variegata,—an ornamental grass.

The pool must be irregular in shape: it may be ovalish, or round at one end and longer and narrower at the other, especially at the point where the bridge is to be placed. (See Fig. 14.) A polythene pool is an excellent choice. (Instructions for making one are given in chapter 7, pages 100–101.)

It is not necessary to plant anything in the pool, the few things required being set at the edge of the water. In the modern Japanese Garden dwarf evergreen trees are the plants mostly used; and few flowers are seen. This scheme may not be to everybody's liking, however. And certainly in a large Japanese Water-garden at least an ornamental Cherry Tree, a Kurume Azalea, some Bamboos and a Japanese Maple should be included.

Rustic bridges are often made by amateur gardeners nowadays. They are best constructed of good, oak planks which may be bought at a timber-yard. Or a single solid piece of wood may be used, each end being fixed firmly in the soil – this type of bridge is common in Japan. (See Fig. 14.)

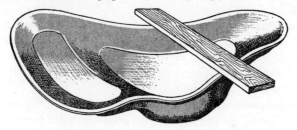

Fig. 14. Fibre-glass for Japanese Water-garden.
Single plank of wood serves as a bridge.

The construction of an arched, stone bridge, which always looks so attractive, especially when it is matured and covered with moss, may need the help of a professional builder. It is well worth the extra money and time spent on it; and it is often possible to get a labourer to give one a hand during the week-end to make and erect it.

Large rocks for setting close to the water-edge are difficult to come by. But the problem may be solved by using four medium-sized ones, roughly the same shape placed together, and forming a reasonably large and regular-shaped boulder. Cement must be used to hold them firmly and permanently in position, and the two at the bottom should be embedded in the soil to a depth of about 3 inches; this is sufficient to give the boulder the appearance of being a natural outcrop-rock.

The ideal site for a Japanese Water-garden is on a gentle slope, the pool, with the bridge, and the rock coming at the bottom. At the top stands the oriental summer-house made of wooden rustic work. Such a garden-house may be bought in sections in attractive cedar-wood and assembled where it is to stand. An oriental touch is given to the building by constructing a curved canopy-like roof for it and by the use of strong Bamboo uprights to support it.

A raked sand bed with rocks in it may be thought by many gardeners to be too austere-looking, and perhaps to Western eyes it is rather colourless; on the other hand it makes a perfect setting for dwarf shrubs or trees grown in pots or earthenware containers. The sanded area need not be larger than an ordinary living-room. One or two rocks, as big as possible, are stood on the sand, which is then raked up into grooves. These grooves or furrows follow the shape of the base of the rocks and extend outward like ripples which appear when water is disturbed. Near the rock is stood a single pot containing perhaps a vivid pink Kurume Azalea or a Japanese dwarfed tree – a Juniper or some other conifer from Japan. A feature like this is actually more oriental in style than a pool with a rock and a bridge and a summer-house above it.

Large Japanese Water-gardens such as those designed in the past for some of our old historic gardens needed a great variety of plants, and there was plenty of room of course for a Tea-house or a Pavilion and other ornaments. The Water-garden at Cliveden, Bucks., has a remarkable collection of plants and a Japanese Pavilion big enough to seat five or six people. The pavilion stands on the top of a mound above a large informal pool. It is an hexagonal building about 12 feet high, made of stone and open on all sides, the curving roof being supported by six stone pillars. They were originally painted blue and attractively gilded. The interior is similarly decorated in blue and gold. From the Pavilion one gets a good view of the rest of the garden. The bridge is simply two huge blocks of sandstone, each about 3 feet wide and 10 or 12 feet long. They do not meet in the middle of the pool, but their ends lie side by side, so that you step from one to the other half-way across the water.

Two varieties of Water-lilies grow in the pool – the rose-crimson JAMES BRYDON with purplish-green leaves and the double, white GONNÊRE (see chapter 4) and among them swim huge Golden Orfe – several 18 inches or more in length.

There is an astonishing variety of Japanese plants growing in the surrounding garden. Japanese Ornamental Cherries; a Japanese Maple, with bronzy-red, Fern-like foliage which turns vivid scarlet in the autumn (3 specimens are planted close together in front of the Pavilion). There are Paeonies, Lilies, Day Lilies (Hemerocallis): PINK PRELUDE and ILLINOIS are two of many varieties; *Primula florindae* on the banks and also growing in the water; several big clumps of *Gunnera manicata*, the Prickly Rhubarb, with leaves 8 feet or more wide; Bamboos in the background and a fine specimen of the Chinese *Thuja orientalis flagelliformis*, with its extraordinary, hanging, cord-like foliage.

A tree this size cannot of course be grown in a limited space; but I think one of the Ornamental Cherries is an excellent choice for any small Japanese Water-garden.

There is a great variety of these hybrid trees, nearly all from Japan, and very popular with gardeners there. They have fascinating names like: ARIAKE (Dawn); FUGENZO (Goddess on a White Elephant); HOKUSAI (Famous Japanese Artist); HORINJI (Ancient Temple in Kyoto); KWANZAN (Named for a Japanese Mountain); OJOCHIN (Large Lantern); TAIZAN-FUKUN (God of Taizan Mountain); WASHINO-O (Eagle's Tail).

All these are beautiful trees for the spring and all of moderate size – some, indeed, not much above 10 or 12 feet. ARIAKE grows about 10 feet tall, the upright branches becoming more spreading with age. The flowers, single or semi-double (pink in the bud and turning flesh colour) open flat and are 2 inches across. It is very similar to OJOCHIN in appearance, which, however, makes a bigger tree. ARIAKE is a good Cherry for growing near a small pool in a Water-garden.

FUGENZO is said to have been in existence at least a thousand years and give a magnificent display of deep rose-pink blossom. It likes cool conditions and prospers in northern gardens.

HOKUSAI. One of the earliest to bloom. It has loose clusters of semi-double, pale pink flowers, hanging on long, thread-like stems. It makes a tall tree with bronzy-red foliage.

HORINJI is a small tree with erect thick branches. It reaches a height of about 12 feet and carries clusters of drooping flowers, semi-double or full double. The outer petals are deep pink; the centre ones a paler shade.

KWANZAN. Described by many growers as the favourite among the coloured Japanese Cherries. A vigorous tree 25 feet or more in height. The flowers come in great abundance; they are large, full-doubled, deep pink in the bud, ageing to rose-red, and at their best in early May.

TAIZAN-FUKUN has smallish fragrant flowers, double and pale pink. The tree is upright in habit and useful for a restricted space.

WASHINO-O. A beautiful Japanese Cherry with outward-pointing branches and clusters of single, fragrant pinkish-white flowers. A well-known planting scheme in gardens is to use this Cherry as a canopy tree for a mass of deep pink or salmon-coloured Azaleas which bloom at the same time.

Japanese Cherries like loamy soil and full sun. If you plant Azaleas under them, you should dig in plenty of sifted leaf-mould or peat where they are to grow and mulch them every April with a 6-inch layer of half-decomposed leaves or coarse leaf-mould.

In a sanded Japanese-garden plant a single specimen of one of these Cherries by a rock. The effect is startling.

Japanese Maples (*Acer*) are tiny shrubs not more than a few inches high when we buy them, and they retain their dwarf habit for many years. They are among the slowest growing of all shrubs and trees.

The type plant, from which the garden forms have originated, is *Acer palmatum*, which grows more quickly than its numerous varieties. It is not so widely planted as they, nor so beautiful. Among the slowest growing is *Acer palmatum* var. RIBESIFOLIUM, one of the best of the dwarf Maples that have come from Japan. The leaves are deeply and finely cut and a dark green which turns old gold in October.

The usual way of planting these dwarf Maples to give a more immediate effect of dense foliage is to set three together in the form of a triangle, one at each angle. In years to come they will grow into a mound, rather flat-topped and elongated – perhaps a little artificial-looking, but very striking. *A.p.* var. DISSECTUM is a bushy, very slow-growing weeping Acer, only a few feet tall. It has dark green finely dissected leaves and is an excellent shrub for growing at the edge of a pool or for planting near a rock. Its common name is Japanese Umbrella Maple. Equally beautiful, and given the same popular name, are var. DISSECTUM ATROPURPUREUM with fern-like deep red leaves; and var. DISSECTUM ORNATUM with green leaves suffused with red, which become deep scarlet early in the autumn.

One of the best autumn-colouring Japanese Maples is the species *Acer nikoense*, which is a slow grower and seldom seen much above 10 feet tall in our gardens. To do really well, it needs deep, moist, leafy soil and partial shade. David Fairchild, the plant collector, grew it in his garden in America and said of it: 'The loveliest of all the introduced species around the house was *Acer nikoense*, a Maple from Japan and Central China. Its delicate leaflets turned to a more beautiful and brilliant scarlet than the autumn foliage of any other Maple I have ever seen.'

All these Maples need a deep, loamy, peaty soil, and since they are very susceptible to late spring frost, must be given a protected spot in exposed gardens.

The genuine Japanese dwarf tress, which are grown in china pots are cultivated specially for indoor decoration. Yet as one of their most important requirements is fresh air, they are excellent plants for a small Japanese Water-garden. They should be put in a conspicuous place, perhaps near a rock in a raked sand garden or area and used instead of an Azalea. The beauty of using these pot plants is that we can change them whenever we feel like it – a dwarf Juniper one day, a vividly coloured Azalea the next, and so on. They are not permanent features. On the other hand we can leave them outside all the winter if we like.

Japanese dwarf trees often suffer through not getting enough fresh air. They are perfectly hardy, and people who possess them should leave them outside for a few hours every day except during exceptionally cold weather.

The best examples have been imported from Japan, and a large variety of trees is used. Not only Conifers, such as Junipers and Pines, but Maples, Beeches, Oaks, Plums, Cherries, Pears and Wisteria. Many are over 100 years old and do not exceed 2 feet in height. Planting them in small, highly-glazed pots helps to restrict the root-run and consequently the development of the stem or trunk.

Subsequent training and pruning are not difficult jobs but they have to be done regularly. The best time for pruning is February, and pinching and twisting of shoots is usually done several times during the summer, and the work is continued till the trees have attained the desired shape. Every fifth year they are repotted and always put into pots the same size. The soil round the bole must be loosened and any very vigorous roots cut away.

But there are many Conifers which are as dwarf as these artificial trees and need no pruning or shaping. True, they ultimately grow into bushes perhaps 3 or 4 feet high but they may take half a century to do it. The miniature Lawson Cypress, *Chamaecyparis lawsoniana nana*, is one of these – there are dozens of others. They are some of the slowest-growing of all shrubs and trees; you can plant them in your youth and you won't see much difference many years later. They are perfect little trees for a small Japanese Water-garden and they are evergreen and therefore interesting all through the year.

There is a charming little Silver Fir, viz. *Abies balsamea* var. HUDSONI with leaves $\frac{1}{4}$ inch long; a native of the White Mountains of New Hampshire. It is about 12 inches high and will take a long time to grow another foot; I have never seen it above 2 feet tall. Plant it near a rock or at the edge of a pool. It likes deep, loamy, moist soil.

Junipers we usually associate with Japan and several lovely forms come from there. *Juniperus procumbens* is the Creeping Juniper from the mountains of Japan and a favourite dwarf conifer for a Water-garden. Although it seldom goes above a height of 18 inches, it spreads out wide, covering the ground for several yards, therefore it mustn't be cramped. Lovely by a pool, the ends of the branches spreading out a little way over the water. Another Juniper, from Central Europe, *J. sabina* var. HUMILIS, known as the Carpet Juniper, is also a dwarf spreading kind, a fine plant for setting near a pool. Care must be taken, however, not to plant it too near, or the mature branches will reach out and almost cover the water, consequently there will be very little room to grow anything in the pool.

As regards planting the pool, a single Water-lily such as the species *Nymphaea tetragona* (found wild in Japan) would be enough. It has olive-green leaves and small white flowers. (See page 68.) It should be planted at the broadest end of the pool, and will give a good show through the summer months. But just as important as a Water-lily are some goldfish and a Japanese Water-garden would not be complete without them.

CHAPTER TWELVE

Some Fish for the Pool

ONE OF the finest collections of goldfish to be seen anywhere in the London district is not in a Water-lily pool, but on the fourth floor of Harrods, Brompton Road, S.W.1. There in a huge glass tank in the Pets' Shop you will see them all sizes and shapes and looking rather overcrowded, though I'm told they are not and that they are very gregarious animals. The striking thing about them is their colour – a glowing warm red-gold. Which is what you don't see when they're swimming about in a pool, and darting among the Water-lilies. Under the glare of the electric light shining through the glass you can enjoy them best. 'Can you eat them?' a little boy once asked me, pressing his finger against the glass. The Chinese are said to eat certain wild kinds, but 'Goldfish' on our menus would doubtless cause one or two gasps.

They are recommended by psychiatrists, however, and used in the therapeutic treatment of nerve cases. Apparently the graceful, flowing movements of the fish induce a state of relaxation and repose. So they say. And when you are in the doldrums, you should go and sit in front of an aquarium.

Outside in the Lily-pool they are a decoration and an enchantment, and their colour, even if it is somewhat subdued, is beautiful to look at.

There is a great variety of goldfish and some of the modern kinds with their extraordinarily decorative fins and tails are not so hardy and tough as the original stocks from which they came. Often the most delicate of them are caught, very carefully in nets, and housed indoors in an aquarium for the winter months. These are what is known as the *Fancy Goldfish* and the ones we usually see swimming about in aquaria.

Although they are crowded together in many of these tanks, they really need plenty of swimming room and for a pool outside we usually state "one inch of fish to one gallon of water.'

Before stocking any pool with fish, however, it is essential to see first that it is in a suitable condition to receive them. A newly constructed cement pool, as I've already mentioned, must be left filled with water for a certain time before it is fit to accommodate either fish or plants. (Chapter 7, page 91.)

Plants to oxygenate the water have been described in previous chapters and they must be growing and well established before they function effectually. Fish should not be put into the water till at least a fortnight after these plants.

Water-lilies, with their canopy-leaves, will provide all the shade necessary for the fish. Other things are required too: rocks should be disposed among the roots of the aquatics for fish to rub against and clean themselves. Not all rocks are suitable, however; they should be of a non-metallic nature and free of limestone. The basaltic type are best.

Food is provided by certain plants such as the Duckweed (*Lemna minor*) and *L. trisulca*, a rampant floating aquatic, best planted in a container; another is the Frogbite (*Hydrocharis morsus ranae*) with small green leaves and tiny white flowers. But before these plants are fully developed and therefore ready to provide food for fish, it may be necessary to use artificial foods, especially in the spring which is the breeding and spawning season. There are many of these foods advertised by fish farms and pet-stores. (Goldfish are omnivorous, feeding on minute crustaceans, worms, snails, fish and a variety of floating and oxygenating plants.) There are pre-packed foods – dried flies, dried *Daphnia*, shredded Shrimp – like our own dehydrated foods. These are packed in polythene bags inside cartons and have full instructions for use.

Daphnia (Water-fleas) are above all the best and most nutritious of live foods and can be caught in nets in natural ponds. They are transparent, rather resembling the ordinary hopping-flea, and may be seen darting and gyrating in hordes in warm sunny places, usually where the water is shallow. If you can't catch any, you can buy them fresh from a pet-shop or a Water-garden nursery.

If you want to breed Goldfish of the best quality and of a true lovely glowing colour, you must buy what the specialists call selected matched breeding pairs. These are in different sizes, varying from 5 inches to 10 inches long. The largest of the hardy Goldfish cost about 50s. a pair.

In the breeding season, as soon as the water is warm enough (usually from May to July), the females release their eggs among the thick plant growth floating near the surface. After the eggs have been fertilized by the males (this happens immediately they have been extruded), they sink and adhere to the leaves of aquatics growing in shallow water and hatch out in about 9 days.

Goldfish are quite hardy and will survive an iced-over pool, provided the surface is broken occasionally to release any toxic gases generated in the water below. And when diseased and dead foliage decomposes, the water naturally becomes contaminated. Hence it is essential to remove all dying leaves and decaying stems in the autumn before winter begins. If the pool is a clean, salubrious place, and the food good, wholesome and reasonably plentiful during the spring and the summer months, Goldfish in captivity will retain their lovely colouring and live for 25 years or more.

The original fish from which our ornamental varieties were derived is a native of Chinese freshwaters, where it is not gold or reddish-gold, but a dull, greenish bronze colour. (Its specific name is *Carassius auratus*.) But golden sports or mutant forms were discovered among them and these were used by Chinese as long ago as the fourth century A.D. to produce a race of ornamental kinds to beautify garden ponds and pools. They were introduced into Japan in 1500 and from there reached Europe and America some 200 years later.

Goldfish are now obtainable in many colours. Some are a golden-red, others may be white or white marked with different colours; yet others are silver or jet black. They are all beautiful. Similarly there is much diversity in their shapes and forms. The Veiltails have large three-lobed drooping tail fins; Lionheads have a swollen wig-like growth on their heads; and there are Telescope-eyed Veiltails, with protruding eyes, and many other kinds. A great number were bred in Japan and have become very popular with collectors and aquarists today; but they have not ousted the well-known golden varieties which came originally from China.

Those we mostly see in our pools are red-gold in colour and normally shaped fish, with no long, drooping, flowing tails. They are graceful and lovely and completely hardy. They vary in size when we buy them from the Fish Farms, the smallest being about 3 inches long; the biggest 6 or 8 inches. They cost from about 1s. 6d. each up to 15s. or so for the biggest kinds.

There are, however, several popular hardy varieties of Fancy Goldfish which will live in outdoor pools all the year round; and perhaps the one liked best and most often seen is the *Shubunkin*, which was bred in Japan at the beginning of the century. It will live for about 12 years and eventually reach a length of 8 inches. It has transparent or non-shining scales. These give a mother-of-pearl effect to the colouring, which is usually a mixture of red, black, brown, yellow and mauve. These colours predominate in the best kinds. The true blue variety (a Kingfisher blue) is extremely rare and much sought after by Goldfish fanciers. The *Shubunkin* is very much like the ordinary Goldfish in shape, and settles down well with them in an outside pool, though some gardeners think it safer indoors in a tank during exceptionally cold winters. The smallest specimens, 2 to 3 inches long, cost 2s. each. (Similarly the Telescopic-eyed Black Moor is a Fancy Goldfish which does well in the warmer pools of our southern gardens. It is a beautiful, jet-black, double-tailed fish, with protruding eyes.)

As hardy as the common Goldfish and the *Shubunkin* is the variety called the *Comet*, with an abnormally long tail and very graceful finnage. A *tour de force*, collectors say, of the fish breeder's art. It is the fastest swimmer of all Goldfish. Small specimens, 3 to 4 inches long, cost 5s. each.

The *Nymph* is a sport from the Veiltails but a hardier fish; the body is thicker, the tail held straight out and often forked. It is quite safe outside in a pool all the winter but lovely enough for the indoor tropical aquarium.

The Golden Orfe was introduced into Britain from Austria where it is more popular than the common Goldfish. Orfe are surface-swimmers and therefore more visible to the spectator than other ornamental fish. They have long, narrow bodies, mature specimens often measuring 2 feet in length. Their colour is salmon-orange; and they flash and dart through the water like streaks of gold. Being surface-feeders, they are useful for controlling insects and snapping up flies that hover over the pool during the summer. The smallest specimens, 1 to 3 inches long, cost half a crown.

Silver varieties are less popular, it seems; the reason for this is that gold shows up better; moreover it is a richer colour and often assumes a reddish-glow in water. In a cloudy pool silver is sometimes scarcely visible.

Although Silver Orfe are not showy, they are beautiful, and the silver and the gold are particularly striking when seen together swimming in shoals near the surface.

Golden and Silver Rudd are both seen occasionally in large ornamental pools and lovely to watch with their reddish tinted fins. They are surface feeders like Orfe; more suitable for big pools and liked by many people because they are easy to tame and will take food from their fingers.

Tench are used mostly as scavenger fish; their colour varies from goldish-green to a rich bronzy gold colour. They are introduced into pools for their useful habit of cleaning up the remains of food left by other fishes and the remains of creatures such as worms which have died in the pool. They are of no decorative value as they avoid light and live as deep down in the water as they can.

The common Green Tench is obtainable from most Fish Farms, the smallest (3-inch size) costing about 3s. 6d. each.

In most small and medium-sized pools today we see usually the common Goldfish, and only a few of them and wisely never overcrowded. Good, healthy fish bought from a reliable dealer will live for many years in a pool where healthy plants grow and prosper.

Goldfish are naturally subject to different kinds of diseases, as are all living organisms, but these are extremely difficult to diagnose for the obvious reason that the fish are seldom still. Sometimes in the evening, however, when they are quiescent it is possible to examine them more closely.

Such troubles as Anchor Worm, Fin Rot and most other diseases that attack fish are all amenable to treatment, provided an early diagnosis is possible.

It is wise to get the advice of an expert when a fish is beginning to show signs of lost vitality. The best way to examine the fish is to take them out of the pool. This is not a difficult job: they can be removed with a net – it could be done once a year – and put into a glass container or a tank where they can be watched for a time and more easily examined.

CHAPTER THIRTEEN

Some More Plants for Pools and Water-Gardens

AQUATICS ARE special plants like Alpines and Cactus, all thriving best in certain places and under certain conditions. No doubt a chalet-garden high up in the Alps would produce the finest show of Alpines, and a garden in North Africa the finest Cactus and desert flowers. Aquatics grow in water or near water, which most of us can supply: true, there are some, *Cabomba caroliniana*, for instance, that need *lime-free* water; but usually these more difficult things are on the tender side and have to be grown in an indoor aquarium – this so-called 'spawning-grass' may be grown outside if it is treated as an annual; it is perhaps useful in pools and ponds stocked with Goldfish. Like the tender *Nymphaea* (Water-lilies, described in chapter 5, it would have to be renewed every year.

The following supplementary list of plants contains aquatics such as *Nymphaea* and other floating plants; ornamental Reeds and Rushes; and herbaceous perennials and one or two flowering shrubs which like deep, moist soils.

Acorus calamus is the Sweet Flag, a native of Britain, 2 to 3 feet tall, with long, sword-shaped leaves and green-yellow flowers in a sheath-like spike. The variety VARIEGATUS, with leaves striped cream and yellow, is more handsome and a better garden plant.

A. gramineus var. VARIEGATUS, with Iris-like leaves striped white is another equally beautiful. Both spread rapidly. The latter is sometimes grown in fountain-pools.

Plant *Acorus* in shallow water near a pool edge, or on a ledge in the pool. Most gardeners use a basket or a container, setting the rhizomes in ordinary loamy soil. (These aquatics cost about 3s. each.)

Alisma gramineum. An aquatic which grows both submerged or at the waterside. In water the leaves are long; but on land they are spoon-shaped and lie flat on the soil in rosettes. The flowers, pinkish-white, come in clusters and bloom in summer. It is a native of Europe, including Britain. (Common names of *Alisma* are Water Plantain and Diel's Spoon.)

Alisma plantago-aquatica (2 to 3 feet tall) is known as the Great Water Plantain. It is the most ornamental species available from nurseries. A native plant with small pale rose flowers in panicles in July, and large, ribbed leaves, resembling those of a Plantain. Shallow water is best for it.

Anagallis tenella is the Bog Pimpernel, a trailing plant, a native, with rose-pink flowers, bell-shaped and about ½ inch wide. They come on stems 4 inches long and bloom in summer. A lovely plant for the Bog-garden or for a pool side. Hillier stocks it at 3s. a root.

Aponogeton krauseanus has been called the loveliest of all the Water Hawthorns. The tubers are best planted in a container in shallow water (4 to 9 inches deep) on a ledge. The leaves are strap-shaped, deep green in colour; and the flowers small, creamy-white, very dainty and stand up several inches out of the pool. They are fragrant and bloom all the summer.

A. ulvaceous is a beautiful aquatic, with sulphur-white flowers and waved, crimped foliage. Too tender for outside pools and recommended for an indoor aquarium stocked with Fancy Goldfish.

Arundo donax, the Provence Reed, a native of southern Europe, common in the Mediterranean region, where its stout canes grow 10 or 12 feet high, often much more. It has large glaucous leaves and panicles (12 to 24 inches long) of brownish-white flowers in late summer. The plant is best grown by the waterside in good deep loam in a sunny sheltered spot. Should be protected during the winter by thick layers of leaves. The common name of *Arundo* is Reed-Grass.

Athyrium filix-femina is the hardy Lady Fern which we sometimes come across growing wild in our moist shady woods. It reaches a height of 3 feet in deep leaf-mould and has vivid green fronds, light and graceful. There are very many attractive varieties, some with broader fronds; others more arching; all of them beautiful. These Ferns could be grown among tall Primulas as foil plants. They thrive with their roots in shallow water, but like drier conditions during the winter.

Brasenia schreberi is one of the rarer aquatics and difficult to establish in many gardens. It should be grown at the edge of a pool or on a ledge in shallow water. The flowers are purple, about ½ inch wide and close up and lie on the surface of the water at night. The leaves, ovalish and small and floating have their submerged parts covered with a gelatinous substance. The plant is known as the Water Shield or Water Target. In North America it is found growing wild in water 4 feet or more deep – usually in lakes; sometimes in slow moving streams and rivers.

Butomus umbellatus, commonly known as the Flowering-Rush, is a native plant and one of the most attractive of our wildings. It grows about 3 feet tall in gardens and has long, sharp-edged leaves and rose-coloured flowers on tall, prominent stems. Stems and foliage are juicy but often damage the mouths of cattle which feed on them. An excellent aquatic for Bog-gardens, the waterside or for growing in quite shallow water. Most nurseries stock it. A root costs about 3s.

Calla palustris, the Bog Arum, has a small, white Arum-like flower and heart-shaped leaves. Not a striking plant (about 6 inches tall) except when grown in a mass, say, along the waterside or in the Bog-garden, if it is a large one. More attractive in the autumn when it bears clusters of scarlet berries. It may be grown in a few inches of water.

Cyperus longus, known as the English Galingale, is an excellent ornamental Grass or Reed and very useful for planting at the edge of a small pool or pond where there is no room for a Bamboo. It makes tufts of grass-like stems and leaves with terminal clusters of brownish-red spikelets. Height: about 3 to 4 feet.

Gunnera manicata (the Prickly Rhubarb) is a giant waterside foliage plant suitable only for growing on the banks of the largest pools and on riverside banks. It is too big for a stream and for any small gardens. The leaves in shape resemble those of the edible Rhubarb and are the largest of any plant we grow in this country.

This species does best in the warmest regions of Britain. In Devon you may see old specimens making clumps 30 feet or more in circumference. Many of these noble-looking plants have 20 or 30 leaves each and the clumps are at least 8 feet high. Some people who grow *G. manicata* leave the flower-panicles to develop; but if they are cut off in the spring, the leaves grow much larger.

In gardens in the London district this gargantuan foliage plant requires a position sheltered from strong, cold winds and some protection during severe winters. It is usually sufficient to pile up the dead leaves and some Bracken or other lightish material over it and leave it covered till the following May when new growth commences. A good specimen costs about 25s.

G. chilensis is not so big as *G. manicata*, but it is really only suitable for very large gardens. Its leaves usually measure from 5 to 6 feet across, and the stems are about 4 feet high. It is less prickly than the bigger plant and does well in rather drier situations. It thrives wonderfully on a river bank which is well above the water level.

Both species need a rich loamy soil, containing well-rotted manure and plenty of leaf-mould. And it should never dry out during the summer and the growing season. When planting them near an informal pool, see that the crowns are set well above the water level in winter so that they are dry during that period. They often suffer much damage if stagnant moisture collects round them during frosty weather.

The smallest species is *G. magellanica*, a miniature of creeping habit, a native of Chile, a useful plant for the edge of a small pool, where it forms a mat of dark green leaves 2 inches across. It is an excellent choice too for a damp spot in a rockery or for planting at the edge of a Bog-garden. It spreads rapidly in damp, peaty soils.

Yet another miniature species is *G. hamiltoni*, which forms broad patches of flattened rosettes 3 or 4 inches across. A fascinating little foliage plant for covering or partly covering a slope in a Water-garden.

Hemerocallis are the Day Lilies which are often seen growing on the banks of a stream or massed on sloping banks leading down to a pool (as in the Japanese Garden at Cliveden, Bucks.). As the popular name suggests, the flowers (Lily-like) are ephemeral and one has to catch them in bloom round about midday to enjoy their full beauty. (The word *Hemerocallis* is from the Greek *hemera*, a day; *kallos*, beauty.) The flowers give a good show, however, coming successionally through June and July; and the long, narrow Rush-like leaves are very decorative in spring and autumn and suggest the waterside. Various kinds have been mentioned in chapter 11, page 147. One of the newest is var. SALADIN, 3 feet tall, with flowers almost cherry-red in colour. At its best in June.

One of the later blooming Day Lilies is *H. thunbergii* with charming light yellow flowers. At the moment it is a little difficult to get.

Plant *Hemerocallis* in deep, loamy, leafy soil. They don't mind wet ground, provided it is very well drained.

Heracleum mantegazzianum (named to commemorate Paola Mantegazzi – 1831 to 1920 – Italian anthropologist). Another giant waterside plant like *Gunnera maniculata*. Its popular name is the Cartwheel Flower – the plant is not often seen in gardens. Its size no doubt deters most people from growing it. It is twice as big as a man and can be used only in a wild garden or as a background plant in a large Water-garden. It is excellent associated with some of the bigger Bamboos by the side of a large pool. The thick stems are topped with large white flowers which come in flattish umbels, the biggest 4 feet or more across. But it is the deeply divided leaves, 3 feet long, which are its great attraction. The plant needs deep moist loam to attain really giant proportions and not many gardens can give it the right setting. Seedlings spring up all over the place where the plant grows and can be something of a nuisance. It is a wise precaution to cut off the 'cartwheel' heads as they begin to fade.

Hosta or *Funkia*. These handsome foliage-plants are often listed in catalogues under the second name. They are commonly known as Plantain Lilies and lovely cool-looking plants for the waterside. (They give a cool refreshing look to a herbaceous border and should be grown there in the front row.) They do better in shade in such a place; but in the Water-garden, where their roots can get down to plenty of moisture, they thrive in sun. Mass planting is most effective.

H. fortunei, a native of Japan, has leaves about 8 inches long and 6 inches wide, and they are not so glaucous as those of *H. glauca*. The variety MARGINATA-ALBA has leaves which are margined with white. This Hosta gives a superbly beautiful effect when massed in a woodland clearing, or in a semi-wild spot as it is in the Japanese Water-garden at Cliveden.

H. glauca has glaucous blue-green leaves, 12 inches long and about 9 inches across. It is widely grown and much admired for its delightful shade of green and the beautiful veining of the leaves. (The conspicuous veining in the *Hosta* is one of their great charms.) A native of Japan. Introduced in 1830.

There are several other species and varieties and all are excellent foliage plants for the Water-garden. Their flowers, tubular and usually a shade of pale lavender (sometimes they are white) are not striking and don't last long. *Hosta* are grown specifically for their lovely, cool-looking leaves. The plants cost about 5s. each.

Hypericum elodes, Marsh St. John's Wort, a small tufted plant with creeping, rooting stems, and branches from 4 to 12 inches high; the leaves are oval and about ¾ inch long; the flowers come in terminal clusters and are pale yellow. A useful creeping plant, never above 6 inches high, and valuable for growing near the water in an artificial pool, where it will hide any ugly cement edge that may be visible. This charming herbaceous perennial may be obtained from Hillier and most nurseries for about 3s. a root.

Juncus nodus (the Knotted Rush) is a fine ornamental Rush for a Bog-garden. The stems vary from 6 to 18 inches in height and in summer carry spiky heads of reddish-brown flowers.

Kalmia latifolia is the Mountain Laurel, an evergreen shrub from North America and prized for its lovely clusters of small pink flowers which come in May and June. The shrub, when in full bloom, rather resembles a Rhododendron and like the Rhododendron family thrives in partial shade and deep, moist peaty soils. A wonderful sight in a large Water-garden, massed on a bank, where there is a certain amount of shade. A beautiful effect is obtained by planting them in such a place and, in a pool below, some deep pink Water-lilies such as MARLIACEA CARNEA. (Described in chapter 4, page 66.)

Miscanthus (from the Greek *miskos*, stem; *anthos*, flower; alluding to the stalked spikelets of the panicles). A genus of ornamental Grasses with attractive plumes; in *M. sinensis* they are about 12 inches long, white tinged with red, and come in September. The leaves, 2½ to 3 feet long and ½ inch wide, are blue-green with a white stripe. This species makes a large clump in time and is a graceful plant for growing as a single specimen against a large pool. There are several excellent varieties such as var. VARIEGATUS with cream, longitudinal stripes (it is not as tall as the type); and ZEBRINUS, a more striking plant with yellow bars running across the leaves.

The species *M. sacchariflorus* is not so often seen. A tall, graceful, Japanese species, which in deep, moist loam will reach a height of 8 feet. the variety AUREUS has its leaves striped with gold.

F

Miscanthus are often listed as *Eulalia* in catalogues and are still called *Eulalia* by many gardeners who grow them. They are completely hardy and best divided up every third or fourth year.

Myriophyllum prosperpinacoides, the Parrot's Feather, a half-hardy aquatic often used for a Fountain basin, where looks very charming hanging over the side, with the water splashing around. It is sometimes grown as an ornamental floating-plant in cool greenhouse pools; and it can also be planted in a pool outside and carefully lifted and planted in an aquarium for the winter. Very attractive with some of the Fancy Goldfish. Its whorls of small, finely-divided leaves come crowded on the stems, which grow about 6 inches out of the water. A delightful and graceful plant. Its roots must be set firmly in a deposit of fibrous loam in shallow water. (The generic name is from *myrios*, a myriad; and *phyllon*, leaf, alluding to the finely divided foliage.)

Nymphaea are the loveliest of all the floating plants we can grow, providing us with a magnificent show of flowers outside in our pools; and indoors there are the tropical kinds, with their flowers on stems raised well out of the water and beautiful and long-lived as cut-flowers. In a warm greenhouse many of them will bloom all the winter.

Some of these were described in chapter 5, pages 76–80. Others – day-blooming hybrids – are:

A. SIEBERT is a free-flowering, rose-coloured variety which is often treated as an annual and grown outside in a pool during the summer months. It was raised by Henkel at the beginning of the century.

AUGUST KOCH may also be planted outside, though more often than not it is grown in a greenhouse because the flowers bloom all the winter. They are a charming shade of blue and make excellent cut-flowers. This Water-lily is one of the viviparous varieties and easily increased. (See page 62.)

BLUE BIRD, another viviparous form with lovely flowers a shade of deep blue.

COLONEL LINDBERGH is one of the best of the indoor day-blooming varieties. Its deep blue flowers are carried on long stems and stand up well above the water. Magnificent for cutting. The flowers, too, are delightfully fragrant.

WILLIAM STONE has large violet-blue flowers with a suggestion of purple in them. They are carried on long thick stems and bloom throughout the day.

Of the night-flowering hybrids the following half a dozen are among the most beautiful it is possible to grow in warm indoor tanks.

BISSETII. Cup-shaped flowers sometimes as much as 10 inches wide; they are double and of a deep rose-red colour. The bronzy-red leaves are extremely attractive and provide an excellent background for the flowers.

JAMES GURNEY, JUNIOR. Deep crimson flowers which become purple in colour as they age.

KEWENSIS. Raised at Kew Botanic Gardens at the end of the last century and is a favourite night-blooming Water-lily both here and in the U.S.A. The flowers are an exquisite shade of pale pink.

MADAME AUGUSTE TEZIER. An uncommonly beautiful Water-lily; the blooms at night, under artificial lighting, are violet-purple in the centre and fade in colour outwards to the edge of the petals. The stamens are brown, and the foliage purplish. A magnificent hybrid raised by Lagrange in 1914.

MARIE LAGRANGE another night-blooming hybrid raised by the same firm. Lovely flowers with white lines marking the centres of the petals, which are rosy-purple. The yellow stamens enhance the beauty of the colouring.

O'MARANA. Raised by Bisset. It has large flowers; some are 12 inches across. The flowers are rose-red and the stamens deep orange-yellow; the foliage deep green. A free-flowering hybrid and very beautiful at night.

Parnassia are hardy perennials suitable for moist, peaty soils, and they flourish luxuriantly in Bog-gardens. They are often found growing near the water in shady or semi-shady places along our river-banks. *P. palustris*, called the Common Grass of Parnassus, is a native species with white flowers, the petals of which are veined with green stripes. The leaves are heart shaped and a shining green colour. It likes boggy places and is a pretty flower for growing on the banks of a natural stream.

Peltiphyllum peltatum, the Umbrella Plant, is a hardy perennial with leaves 6 to 12 inches across, which are carried on stems 2 feet long. The flowers, small, white or pink, come in spring before the leaves. The plant makes a fine mass of flat foliage (bright green above and paler beneath) for the Water-garden.

L. H. Bailey, the American horticulturist, describes the plant under *Saxifraga peltata* and says it is: 'Hardy in Massachusetts, with slight protection, and a most desirable plant where bold effects are wanted.' It may be seen at Kew Botanic Gardens, on the banks of the lake, associated with the giant *Gunnera manicata*, described on page 158. And the variety NANA (dwarf) grows at the foot of a boulder near water in the rockery at Kew, its flat roundish leaves harmonizing well with the grey rocks.

Petasites japonica, another hardy perennial, has flat leaves 3 to 4 feet across, which provide good, bold clumps in the Water-garden. The flowers, purplish-white, bloom in February; the plant is therefore much valued by gardeners for its early spring show. The variety GIGANTEA is larger and in rich damp soil reaches a height of 6 feet. In Japan, where it grows wild, the stems are cooked and eaten as a vegetable, or served, with sugar, as a dessert.

Phalaris arundinacea variegata is an ornamental Grass rather resembling the lovely *Glyceria aquatica variegata* (see page 110). Its leaves are ¾ inch wide, with thin white stripes, and are highly decorative in spring. Later on the flowering stems go up to a height of from 2 to 5 feet and carry small panicles of greenish purple spikelets. A good grass for planting at the edge of a pool where the soil is moist and loamy. The popular name is Ribbon Grass or Gardener's Garters. It can be bought from Hillier for about 3s.

Phormium tenex is the New Zealand Flax, a valuable evergreen plant, which forms a clump of rigid, leathery and slightly glaucous leaves, varying from 3 to 9 feet in length. The flowers are bronzy-red and are carried in panicles as much as 15 feet tall. Each flower is from 1 to 2 inches long and tubular in shape. The plant is scarcely hardy enough for gardens near London but it can be seen occasionally in this district growing in ornamental pools. About the end of May the root-stock is simply set in good turfy loam in a large container and sunk in shallow water. It is very handsome grown in this way, and during a hot summer will flower freely. Before the frosts come, the plant is lifted and taken into the greenhouse, where it is kept in sandy leaf-mould till the following spring.

In our warm southern gardens this *Phormium* is usually quite safe through the winter months; but when an exceptionally cold spell is expected, some sort of protective material should be rigged up round the clumps, such as several stout stakes driven into the ground round the plants and sacking tied to them to form a sort of open-top tent.

Pogonia ophioglossoides is one of the hardiest of the *Pogonia*, a race of Orchid-like plants which are sometimes seen in a bed of Sphagnum moss and peat in a sheltered part of the Water-garden. The flowers are fragrant and rose-coloured. The soil must be well drained and some slight protection may be necessary during severe winters.

Polystichum lonchitis, the Holly Fern, a hardy native species, which is very popular with gardeners and often grown in a pot for indoor decoration. It is small enough for growing among rocks against a tub-sized pool and will often be found in such a place. An excellent foil plant for some of the waterside Primulas. The fronds are densely tufted, usually about 12 or 18 inches high and about 3 inches wide. It is a choice little Fern for the Water-garden and costs about 8s. 6d. a root.

Rheum, like the *Gunnera*, have been compared with the edible Rhubarb. The common name is Ornamental Rhubarb and they are among the most handsome of the large-leaved foliage-plants. They will doubtless appeal to gardeners who haven't room for the giant *Gunnera manicata*.

The best one for the Water-garden, and about the only one obtainable from nurseries, is *Rheum palmatum*, with deeply-lobed leaves on long stems. It forms a thick mound of foliage, from which stand up the tall flower-stems carrying long, large panicles of deep red flowers.

There are several varieties which are offered by nurseries, viz. TANGUTICUM, which has larger leaves, more deeply lobed than the type plant. Var. ATROSANGUINEUM and BOWLES' CRIMSON have tall, upright crimson flower-panicles which are ideally set-off by the deep green, flat leaves.

Some fine specimens of these plants may be seen in semi-woodland at the Savill Gardens, Windsor.

These plants like partial shade and benefit much from an annual mulching of sifted peat or leaf-mould.

Rodgersia is another class of large-leaved foliage-plants. They need, as do *Gunnera* and *Rheum*, deep moist leafy loam such as they get in a Water-garden. About half a dozen species are offered by nurseries. Those I have come across most frequently in this district are the following:

Rodgersia aesculifolia with large handsome leaves consisting of 5 radiating leaflets (like those of a Horse Chestnut leaf). They are of a rich russet-brown colour and are carried on long, slender stems. In the Savill Gardens you can see this plant in April shooting up through the moist leafy soil. The foliage is fresh and beautiful then. In summer the flowers, white, come in large clusters on stems about 2 feet tall. The habitat of the plant is China. Good specimens can be obtained for about 7s. 6d. a root.

R. pinnata has leaves with 5 to 9 leaflets, which are about 6 inches long and half as wide, and the flowers are an attractive shade of red. The variety SUPERBA is a superior garden-plant, I think, and has long panicles of rich pink flowers.

R. podophylla was the first species to be introduced into cultivation and has leaves, 5-foliate, measuring 6 to 18 inches across. The flowers are yellowish-white and come in large panicles in July. A well-grown clump after some years often measures 8 or 9 feet in diameter. An imposing foliage-plant for the waterside. The brownish-red colour of the leaves lasts well and assumes a more intense hue in the sun. The plant is a native of Japan and was introduced into Britain in 1880.

Schizostylis coccinea. Its common names are Caffre Lily, and Crimson Flag. This is a South African bulbous plant, best grown in our warmer southern gardens. It rather resembles a *Gladiolus*, with its narrow, sword-like leaves and clusters of scarlet flowers at the top of the stem. It blooms late – in September as a rule – and will flourish in deep peaty soils in Water-gardens in districts where there is little or no frost. It grows about 2 feet tall.

Scirpus cernuus is one of the ornamental Rushes and like the Caffre Lily suitable only for very sheltered gardens and even there is perhaps best lifted in the autumn and grown on in a frost-proof greenhouse. (See page 125.) Its drooping, hair-like, grass stems are quite extraordinary and artificial-looking. It is a favourite pot plant for edging shelves in the conservatory.

Spiranthes cernua is a hardy terrestrial Orchid which blooms fairly late in the season and comes from the swamps and bogs of North America. It has sweetly-scented small white flowers which are carried in spikes from 2 to 5 inches long. The leaves are long and narrow. The stems measure up to 30 inches in length. A pretty plant for damp soils containing lime-rubble.

Wisteria. These flowering climbers or vines are the loveliest of Waterside plants and most effective perhaps when the long twining stems are trained over a bridge and the clusters of lavender-blue flowers hang down to touch the water. Claude Monet grew the plants on a bridge in his Water-garden at Giverny, as mentioned in chapter 3.

When the plants grow old, their stems get very thick and woody – like tree trunks – and are too heavy for most wooden bridges. Wisteria are best trained against stonework or on walls. In some Water-gardens (at Cliveden, for instance) various kinds are grown as standards and kept to about 5 feet in height. The stems are then heavy with flowers and make a very beautiful picture.

W. floribunda var. ALBA with white hanging racemes up to 2 feet long is a good plant for training in this way. It should be pruned back hard annually in winter; and in August given a second pruning, which should consist of a mere shortening back of the leafy shoots. The type plant, *W. floribunda* (Japanese Wisteria), with its long, violet or purplish-blue racemes, delightfully fragrant, may be pruned in the same way.

The soil should be a deep, moist loam containing plenty of sandy leaf-mould or sifted peat and must never be allowed to dry out.

The finest and most floriferous Wisteria will be found in warm sunny gardens in the south.

Flowering shrubs, however, are less important in a Water-garden than plants that grow in water. And the loveliest of them all are the Water-lilies which do as well in northern gardens as they do in the south.

Douglas Bartrum
Sunnyside
Bovingdon Green
MARLOW
BUCKS

BIBLIOGRAPHY

Ascherson (P.) and Gürke (M.) – HYDROCHARITACEAE IN DIE NATÜRLICHEN PFLANZEN FAMILIEN.

Austin (Watson F.) – FISHPONDS AND HOME AQUARIUMS.

Baker (J. G. – HANDBOOK OF THE FERN ALLIES.

Battandier (J. A.) – FLORA DE L'ALGÉRIE.

Bean (W. J.) – TREES AND SHRUBS HARDY IN THE BRITISH ISLES.

Bentham and Hooker – GENERA PLANTARUM.

Caspary (R.) – LES NYMPHÉACÉES FOSSILES. (Ann. des sci. nat. ser.)

Conard (H. S.) – MONOGRAPH OF THE WATER-LILY.

Correvon (H.) – LES ORCHIDÉES RUSTIQUES.

Coste (L'Abbe H.) – FLORE DE LA FRANCE.

Curtis – BOTANICAL MAGAZINE.

Darwin (C.) – INSECTIVOROUS PLANTS.

Edwards – BOTANICAL REGISTER.

Engler (A.) – BOTANISCHE JAHRBÜCHER.

Fox (Wilson G.) – 'SOME PESTS OF WATER LILIES.' (R.H.S. Journal, 1928.)

Freeman (Mitford A. B.) – THE BAMBOO GARDEN.

Fry – BRITISH MOSSES.

Gluck (H.) – SÜSSWASSER FLORA MITTEL EUROPAS.

Gwynne (S.) – CLAUDE MONET AND HIS GARDEN.

Index Kewensis.

Jekyll (G.) – WALL AND WATER GARDENS.

Lawson (G.) – THE ROYAL WATER LILY OF SOUTH AMERICA AND THE WATER LILIES OF OUR OWN LAND.

Lowe (E. J.) – FERNS, BRITISH AND EXOTIC.

Nairne (A. K.) – THE FLOWERING PLANTS OF WESTERN INDIA.

Niklitschek (A.) – WATER LILIES AND WATER PLANTS.

Rendle (A. B.) – NAIADACEAE IN DAS PFLANZENREICH.

R.H.S. Dictionary.

Small (J. K.) – FLORA OF THE SOUTH EASTERN UNITED STATES.

Smith (J.) – DICTIONARY OF ECONOMIC PLANTS.

Stout (A. B.) – DAYLILIES.

Webster (A. D.) – BRITISH ORCHIDS.

INDEX

Abies balsamea var. HUDSONI, 150
Acer
  nikoense, 149
  palmatum, 148
    Var. DISSECTUM, 148
      DISSECTUM ATROPUR-
        PUREUM, 149
      DISSECTUM ORNATUM,
        149
      RIBESIFOLIUM, 148
Acorus
  calamus, 156
    Var. VARIEGATUS, 156
  gramineus
    Var. VARIEGATUS, 156
Adiantum pedatum, 111
Alders, 22, 45
Aldrovanda versiculosa, 127, 128
Alisma
  gramineum, 156
  plantago-aquatica, 157
Alnus (Alder)
  glutinosa, 45
    Var. IMPERALIS, 45
  incana, 45
    Var. AUREA, 45
      LACINATA (ACUMI-
        NATA), 45
  nitida, 45
  rugosa (*serrulata*), 45
Alopecurus pratensis
  Var. AUREUS, 109
    FOLIIS VARIEGATIS, 109
Anacharis canadensis, 114
Anagallis tenella, 157
Andromeda polifolia, 122

Anemone narcissiflora, 131
  nemorosa, 49
  rivularis, 131
Aponogeton
  distachyus, 115
  krauseanus, 157
  ulvaceus, 157
Arctostphylos uva-ursi, 22
Arethusa bulbosa, 122
Arum Lily, 134
Arundinaria
  ancaps, 42
  fastuosa, 42
  japonica, 42
  palmata, 42
Arundo donax, 157
Astilbe, cultivation of, 26
  Varieties of, 26, 27
Athyrium filix-femina, 157
Azaleas, 22
Azolla caroliniana, 115

Bamboos, 42, 43
Betula
  pendula, 22
    Var. PURPUREA, 22
      YOUNGII, 22
Bladderworts, 130
Blechnum
  spicant, 27, 28
  tabulare, 112
Bletilla striata, 122
Bluebells, 40
Bog Arum, 158
Bog-gardens, 118–121
Bogs, 118

Broad Buckler Fern, 43
Brooks and streams, 19–37
Bulrush, 42
Butomus umbellatus, 10, 158

Cabomba caroliniana, 156
Caffre Lily, 166
Calla palustris, 158
Callitriche verna, 114
Caltha palustris, 20, 107
Var. PLENA, 20
Campanula
portenschlagiana, 139
pyramidalis, 139
Carassius auratus (Goldfish), 153
Cardamine pratensis (Milk Maids), 49
Carex morrowii variegata, 109
Carnivorous plants, 127–131
Carpet Juniper, 150
Catalpa bignonioides, 121
Ceratophyllum demersum, 114
Ceterach officinarum, 112
Chamaecyparis lawsoniana nana, 150
Cliveden, 104, 116, 167
Cloud Ponds or Dew Ponds, 88
Concrete Pools, 89
Coreopsis, 131, 132
Cornus
alba, 22
stolonifera, 22
Crimson Flag (Caffre Lily), 166
Cyperus longus, 158
Cypripedium
acaule (humile), 123
calceolus, 123
pubescens (hirsutum), 123
reginae, 118, 123, 124

Dactylis glomerata elegantissima, 109
Daffodils (Trumpet), 39, 40
Darlingtonia californica, 128

Dionaea muscipula, 128
Drosera (Sundews), 128, 129
anglica, 129
longifolia, 129
rotundifolia, 129
Drosophyllum lusitanicum, 129
Dryopteris
dilatata, 43
fili-mas, 28, 31
Var. BOLLANDIAE, 28
oreopteris, 28
thelypteris, 112

Elymus arenarius, 110
English Galingale, 158
Epilobium angustifolium, 59, 60
Erica tetralix, 22
Eurayle ferox, 82

Fancy Goldfish, 151
Ferns, 27–29
Festuca ovina glauca, 110
Filipendula
camtschatica, 132
purpurea, 132
Food for Goldfish, 152
Fountains, 134–137
Funkia (Hosta), 160

Gardener's Garters or Ribbon Grass, 164
Gaultheria, 22
Gentiana verna, 121
Geum rivale, 132
LEONARD'S VARIETY, 132
Glyceria aquatica variegata, 110
Glyptostrobus pensilis, 46
Golden Orfe, 154
Goldfish, 104, 151–155
diseases, 155
Gunnnera
chilensis, 159
hamiltoni, 159
magellanica, 159
manicata, 158

Hemerocallis
  thunbergii, 159, 160
  Varieties, 147
Heracleum mantegazzianum, 160
Holcus mollis variegatus, 110, 111
Hopatcong, 58
Hosta, 160, 161
  fortunei, 160
  glauca, 160
Hottonia palustris, 115
Hyacinths, 40
Hydrangea macrophylla varieties, 23
Hydrocharis morus-ranae, 116
Hypericum elodes, 161

Inula helenium, 132
Iris
  aurea, 106
  cristata, 105, 106
  delavayi, 106
  douglasiana, 106
  foetidissima, 29
  germanica varieties, 56
  graminea, 106
  kaempferi, 29, 30, 106
    Varieties, 30
  laevigata, 29, 30, 106
  ochroleuca Var. QUEEN VICTORIA, 106
  pseudacorus, 21, 29
  pumila, 105
  setosa, 106
  sibirica, 29, 40, 106
    Varieties, 47

Japanese Gardens, 15, 35
Japanese Maples, 148, 149
Japanese Ornamental Cherry Trees, 147, 148
Japanese Water-gardens, 144–150

Juncus
  effusus Var. SPIRALIS, 69
  nodosus, 119
Juniperus
  procumbus, 150
  sabina Var. HUMILIS, 150

Kalmia latifolia, 161
Kirengeshoma palmata, 132, 133
Knightshayes Court, formal pool at, 116
Kniphofia
  macowanii, 30, 31
  uvaria, 31
  Varieties, 31
Knotted Rush, 161

Laburnum × *vossii*, 40
Lady Slipper Orchids, 123, 124
Lawson Cypress, 150
Ledum groenlandicum, 23
Lemna trisulca, 116
Lilium
  canadense, 133
  pardalinum, 133
  superbum, 133
Lobelia
  cardinalis, 133
  Varieties, 133
Lychnis
  chalcedonica, 31, 133
  chalcedonica rubra plena, 31
  coronata sieboldii, 31
  flos-cuculi, 21
  × *haageana*, 31
Lysichitum, 31, 32
  americanum, 32
  camtschatense, 32
Lythrum salicaria, 21, 50
  Varieties, 50

Marsh Marigold, 20
Marsh St. John's Wort, 161
Matteucia struthiopteris, 112

Mentha aquatica, 141
Menyanthes trifoliata, 141, 142
Midelney Place, Water-garden
 at, 103, 117
Mimulus
 luteus, 32
 luteus guttatus, 32
 moschatus, 32
 ringens, 32
Miscanthus,
 sacchariflorus, 161
  Var. AUREUS, 161
 sinensis, 161
 Varieties, 161
Monet's Water-garden, 54–56,
 167
Mountain Laurel, 161
Myosotis
 scorpioides, 20
 scorpioides semperflorens, 20
  Var. *alba,* 20
Myrica gale, 122
Myriophyllum prosperpinacoides, 162

Narcissus 'Pheasant Eye,' 39
 bulbocodium, 48
 Varieties, 48, 49
 cyclamineus, 49
 Varieties, 49
 'Pheasant Eye,' 39
Nasturtium officinale, 49
Nelumbo
 lutea, 62
 nucifera, 13, 62, 63, 83, 84
Nepenthes (Pitcher Plants), 127
New Zealand Flax, 164
Night-blooming *Nymphaea,* 78–
 80
Nitella, 114
Nuphar
 advena, 85
 japonica, 85
  Var. RUBROTINCTUM, 85
 microphylla, 85

Nymph (Fish), 154
Nymphaea
 alba, 11, 57, 62
 amazonum, 76
 ampla, 76
 burtii, 76
 caerulea, 11, 76
 candida, 64
 capensis, 76
 fennica, 65
 gigantea, 77
 lotus, 11, 77
 nitida, 66
 odorata, 66, 67
  Varieties, 67
 pubescens, 77, 78, 84
 pygmaea alba, 67
  × *pygmaea helvola,* 11, 67
 rubra, 78
 stellata, 78
 tetragona, 68
 tuberosa rosea, 68
 Varieties
  LAYDEKERI, 65–66
  MARLIAC HYBRIDS, 62–64,
   65, 66, 67, 68
  night-blooming, 78–80
  tender (species and varieties), 73–80

Onoclea sensibilis, 113, 142
Orchis, 124–127
Ornamental Rhubarb, 165
Osmunda regalis, 28
 Varieties, 28
Ostrich Fern, 112
Oxygenating Plants, 114

Parnassia palustris, 163
Peltiphyllum peltatum, 163, 164
Petasites japonica, 164
Phalaris arundinacea variegata, 164

Phormium tenex (New Zealand Flax), 164
Phyllitis scolopendrium, 113
  Var. CRISPUM GRANDE, 113
Phyllostachys
  ruscifolia, 43
  viridi-glaucescens, 42, 43
Pistia stratiotes, 83
Pitcher Plants, 127
Pogonia ophioglossoides, 165
Polygonum affine, 32, 33
Polystichum setigerum, 113
Polythene Pools, 100, 101
Pools, artificial, 87–104
  puddled, 88, 89
Populus
  heterophylla, 46
  nigra, 46
  × *serotina* Var. AUREA, 46
Potamogeton crispus, 115
Prickly Rhubarb, 158
Primula
  bulleyana, 25
  cockburniana, 25, 26
  denticulata, 51
    Varieties, 51
  florindae, 19, 24, 106
  helodoxa, 25
  japonica, 9, 25, 26
  poissonii, 25
  pulverulenta, 26
  rosea, 19, 24, 120
  sikkimensis, 23, 24, 29, 107
Pterocarya fraxinfolia, 121
Puddled Pools, 88, 89

Ranunculus
  aquatilis, 103, 107
  bullatus, 107
  lingua, 107
Reed Mace, 41, 69
Rheum
  palmata, 165
    Varieties, 165

Rhododendron
  nudiflorum, 22
  viscosum, 22, 46
Ribbon Grass, 164
Rodgersia, 165
  aesculifolia, 166
  pinnata, 166
  podophylla, 166
Rubus arcticus, 23
Rumex hydrolapathum, 20
Rusty-back Fern, 112

Salix
  alba, 44
  babylonica, 21, 44
  × *blanda*, 21
  daphnoides, 44, 45
  × *salamonii*, 44
  vitellina
    Var. BRITZENSIS, 44
      PENDULA, 21
Sarracenia
  drummondi, 130
  flava, 129, 130
  purpurea, 129, 130
Saxifraga peltata (Umbrella Plant), 163, 164
Schizostylis coccinea, 166
Scirpus
  cernuus, 125, 166
  lacustris, 42
  tabernaemontanus zebrinus, 108
Senecio clivorum, 133
Shubunkin (Fish), 154
Silver Orfe, 155
Silver Rudd, 155
Spiraea
  × *arguta*, 33
  crenata, 33
  hypericifolia, 33
  japonica Var. ANTHONY WATERER, 33
  thunbergii, 33
Spiranthes cernua, 166

Stipa pennata, 111
Stratiotes aloides, 116
Swamp Lily, 133

Taxodium distichum, 46, 121
Tench, 155
Trillium grandiflorum, 133, 134
Trollius
   europaeus, 108
   hybridus, 108
   Varieties, 108
Typha
   latifolia, 41
   laxmanni, 109
   minima, 109, 141

Umbrella Plant, 163
Utricularia
   intermedia, 131
   vulgaris, 130, 131

Vaccineum corymbosum, 23
Veiltails (Fish), 154
Venus's Fly-trap, 128
Victoria
   amazonica, 11, 62, 81, 82
   trickeri, 82, 83
Viviparous Water-lilies, 62, 78

Water Chinkapin, 62
Watercress, 48, 49
Water-grass, 119
Water Violet, 115
Willows, 39, 43–45
Wisteria
   floribunda, 55
      Varieties, 55, 167
   sinensis, 55, 56

Zantedeschia aethiopica (Arum Lily), 134

Stipa pennata, 111
Stratiotes aloides, 116
Swamp Lily, 133

Taxodium distichum, 46, 121
Tench, 155
Trillium grandiflorum, 133, 134
Trollius
    europaeus, 108
    hybridus, 108
      Varieties, 108
Typha
    latifolia, 41
    laxmanni, 109
    minima, 109, 141

Umbrella Plant, 163
Utricularia
    intermedia, 131
    vulgaris, 130, 131

Vaccineum corymbosum, 23
Veiltails (Fish), 154
Venus's Fly-trap, 128
Victoria
    amazonica, 11, 62, 81, 82
    trickeri, 82, 83
Viviparous Water-lilies, 62, 78

Water Chinkapin, 62
Watercress, 48, 49
Water-grass, 119
Water Violet, 115
Willows, 39, 43–45
Wisteria
    floribunda, 55
      Varieties, 55, 167
    sinensis, 55, 56

Zantedeschia aethiopica (Arum
    Lily), 134

Phormium tenex (New Zealand Flax), 164
Phyllitis scolopendrium, 113
  Var. CRISPUM GRANDE, 113
Phyllostachys
  ruscifolia, 43
  viridi-glaucescens, 42, 43
Pistia stratiotes, 83
Pitcher Plants, 127
Pogonia ophioglossoides, 165
Polygonum affine, 32, 33
Polystichum setigerum, 113
Polythene Pools, 100, 101
Pools, artificial, 87–104
  puddled, 88, 89
Populus
  heterophylla, 46
  nigra, 46
  × *serotina* Var. AUREA, 46
Potamogeton crispus, 115
Prickly Rhubarb, 158
Primula
  bulleyana, 25
  cockburniana, 25, 26
  denticulata, 51
    Varieties, 51
  florindae, 19, 24, 106
  helodoxa, 25
  japonica, 9, 25, 26
  poissonii, 25
  pulverulenta, 26
  rosea, 19, 24, 120
  sikkimensis, 23, 24, 29, 107
Pterocarya fraxinfolia, 121
Puddled Pools, 88, 89

Ranunculus
  aquatilis, 103, 107
  bullatus, 107
  lingua, 107
Reed Mace, 41, 69
Rheum
  palmata, 165
    Varieties, 165

Rhododendron
  nudiflorum, 22
  viscosum, 22, 46
Ribbon Grass, 164
Rodgersia, 165
  aesculifolia, 166
  pinnata, 166
  podophylla, 166
Rubus arcticus, 23
Rumex hydrolapathum, 20
Rusty-back Fern, 112

Salix
  alba, 44
  babylonica, 21, 44
  × *blanda*, 21
  daphnoides, 44, 45
  × *salamonii*, 44
  vitellina
    Var. BRITZENSIS, 44
      PENDULA, 21
Sarracenia
  drummondi, 130
  flava, 129, 130
  purpurea, 129, 130
Saxifraga peltata (Umbrella Plant), 163, 164
Schizostylis coccinea, 166
Scirpus
  cernuus, 125, 166
  lacustris, 42
  tabernaemontanus zebrinus, 108
Senecio clivorum, 133
Shubunkin (Fish), 154
Silver Orfe, 155
Silver Rudd, 155
Spiraea
  × *arguta*, 33
  crenata, 33
  hypericifolia, 33
  japonica Var. ANTHONY
    WATERER, 33
  thunbergii, 33
Spiranthes cernua, 166